CHI-TOWN GANGSTER

CHAMPAGNE POWELL

Copyright © 2024 Champagne Powell
All rights reserved
First Edition

PAGE PUBLISHING
Conneaut Lake, PA

First originally published by Page Publishing 2024

While this story is inspired by actual persons and events, certain characters, characterizations, incidents, locations, and dialogues were fictionalized or invented for purpose of dramatization.

ISBN 979-8-88960-514-0 (pbk)
ISBN 979-8-88960-527-0 (digital)

Printed in the United States of America

ACKNOWLEDGMENTS

This is dedicated to my father and mother Peter and Frances Powell for their dedication to the provision and protection of their children. I recognize also the support of my brothers and sisters featuring the love we all share. I also recognize my childhood friends deceased or now alive in their 70s, with whom I shared this dangerous Chicago teen history.

PROLOGUE

THE DISCIPLE BLACK STONE WAR

The period of 1965 to 1978, Champagne and his childhood friends experienced an ongoing street battle that pertained ONLY to Chicago. This city was then and even now uniquely considered the most segregated city in the United States. The difference between Chicago Black teenagers and the rest of the country is extensive; examples include the area of dance and what was then called BOPPING morphed into what is now called STEPPING. In the arena of fashion, Chicago teenage gangsters created what was called the GOUSTER dress style. During the 1960s, recording artist David Bowie documented this unique Chicago Black teenager phenomenon. He adapted his version of the style and coronated his upcoming album "GOUSTER."

The innovation of television had a most unique effect upon these Black teenagers of Chicago. Not one invention entered American homes faster than that of black and white television sets. By 1955, at least half of all U.S. homes had one. In 1968, Chicago entertainer Oscar Brown Jr. engaged with talented members of The Blackstone Rangers street gang and created a musical stage show. The show in part was aired nationally on the Smothers Brothers TV show. The episode was aired at 9:30 pm, January 28th,1968. The entire month of January in Chicago is traditionally the coldest month of the year, with an average of 16 days below freezing. Only one day will reach above 50 degrees Fahrenheit. Most teenagers and everyone else were seeking warmth in their homes. Although televisions were in most US homes by 1955, in 1968 images of anyone Black was a real item to those Black families with a television set. Imagine Black teenagers in phenomenal numbers watching teenagers, who looked like themselves on TV residing in their city of Chicago. The Blackstone Rangers, who most teens in Chicago had never heard of, were now instant celebrities. Suddenly, the Ranger's encounters with the Disciples, (who were already known throughout Chicago's Southside), became nightly news. These teenage Rangers, through word of mouth, passed on to all willing to share in the knowledge that they had created a new organization and wished to include all street gangs in what they called their Nation. For those smaller street gangs attempting to protect themselves from The Disciples and their Disciple branches across Chicago, they could strengthen themselves by joining the Black P. Stone Nation.

The attraction did not stop there for this phenom never seen before anywhere in the United States at the time. Of course, there were no membership cards to count members but there was for the first time in Black American teenage history, there was now a uniquely structured and immense teenage organization. There now appeared an organized emblematic structure for teenagers to join, digest and understand. There appeared a structured salute where Black P. Stone members and affiliates recognized each other. This teenage organization, whose true numbers have been drastically misreported by reporting sources, can only be fairly assessed by defining the Black population in those areas of Chicago controlled by them at the time.

Due to the 1970s mass incarceration of Black teen youth imprisoned and not released into this present society of substance use disorder (including a CRACK induced absence of honor and respect), such teenage organizations can no longer exist. The ability to organize is nonexistent without honor and respect. Respect and honor have been replaced with Crack babies and chaos.

There exists today, no longer enmity between these ex-Disciples and Black P. Stone members now in their 70s. The actual and original Black P. Stone Nation was dismantled more or less by 1978. These surviving elders share each other's gratitude for the fact that they have lived this long and wish to enjoy, without violence, the years they have remaining.

This is a story "inspired by real-life events". It follows a youth who at age 15, (after the gang murder of his best friend) is placed in charge of a nearly 300-member teen group composed of his fellow high school students. Logistics have their neighborhood surrounded by two Disciple gang factions. The 15-year-old, called CP, leads his classmates to a meeting uniting with a small street gang in their area. Although his ambition is to become a singer and Hollywood actor, he is locked in a situation he believes must be a priority for his community's survival. After clashes with the Disciples and a search for the Disciple Hitmen in his neighborhood, death and disappointment appear to follow him through the years. CP and those who love him can only pray for a miracle.

FADE IN:

EXT. STREET - NIGHT

CAPTION: s/b SUPER: August 1971, Chicago, Illinois. Two autos park under the elevated train tracks, which cross busy Racine Avenue.

EXT. STREET - SAME NIGHT TEDDY'S RECORD SHOP

Lights turn off as three well-dressed teenagers and Ted, a sharply dressed thirty-year-old male, exit a record shop. The thirty-year-old hands over an envelope to the group leader, twenty-one-year-old LARRY DAVEN, and turns and locks the door behind him. LARRY examines the package with a glance.

>   LARRY
> Come on, you ain't no gangster, we'll take you where you're going. You're paying the right people this time.

>   TED
> Yeah, Larry, I'm a civilian, no gangster. I sell heroin, and I always use the EL to get somewhere.

Ted crosses the street to the elevated train station entrance.

INT. CAR - NIGHT

Seated is CP, aged twenty-one, five feet, eleven inches, black wide-brimmed hat, suit with muscles. CP is singing "Acappella."

> **CP**
> (singing the 1954 hit by Johnny Ace "Never Let Me Go")
>
> > Just let me love you tonight, forget about tomorrow. My darling, won't you hold me tight and never let me go.

CP notes Ted crossing the street to the elevated train station entrance. He sticks his arm outside his car window and gets the attention of car 2 parked behind him. He signals the car and points to Ted.

INT. CAR 2 PARKED BEHIND CP

> **ANDY**
> Go ahead. We'll meet at Ashland.

The driver, Andy, signals CP with a simple finger wave.

Four males exit the vehicle. The fourth is a black Goliath called BIG MAN, wearing khakis, and a wifebeater.

INT. ELEVATED TRAIN - SAME NIGHT

The train doors open. The car has only three passengers, an elderly woman with a nine-year-old girl and a middle-aged male construction worker in deep sleep.

Ted enters, locates a seat at the far end. The first of three teens enters the car. He wastes no time as he walks directly to Ted, punches him in the face without missing a beat. The well-built teen then reaches under Ted's jacket and removes a 32-caliber pistol from Ted's belt.

> **FIRST TEEN**
> Satan Lovers, LOVERSTONE punk!

The SECOND TEEN following the first places a 38 revolver to Ted's forehead.

The THIRD TEEN holds open the car door as the huge bear of a man accompanying them walks in, eyeing Ted lustfully.

> TEEN 2
> Don't move punk! Everybody else get off this train!

The first teen is now holding Ted's pistol, along with his own 22 caliber, and escorts the old woman, child, and construction worker now in shock and fully awake, out of the car.

The doors are allowed to close and the train begins to move.

Ted has a nosebleed.

> TED
> Please! I ain't got nothing on me.
> Y'all Satan Lovers know that! CP knows that!

Teen 1 puts pistols in his belt and quickly removes a thin rope from the pocket of his mid length black leather coat.

> TEEN 1
> We don't know what you got. You could've changed up. Put your hands behind you and stand up!

Teen 2 presses the pistol harder to Ted's forehead. Ted cooperates.

> TED
> Okay! Okay! Check it out. I'm paying Richmond tomorrow. Ain't nobody changed up!

Ted's hands are quickly tied.

TEEN 1
Man, I said we don't know what you've got! You probably hiding it in your draws! Stand up, let me check it out.

Teen 1 unbuckles and pulls down Ted's pants. Teen 1 looks at Teen 2. He tightly binds Ted's legs together.

Teen 2 moves to the rear door with Teen 3. Teen 1 stuffs a handkerchief down Ted's throat and looks at the smiling huge muscle-bound man waiting his turn to engage with their captive.

Teen 1 produces a small jar of Vaseline. He hands it to the waiting giant. He readies his pistols. He moves to the front doors of the elevated car.

TEEN 1
Take care of business, Big Man. Do your thing.

Ted's eyes grow wide. The huge man stares at Ted lustfully as if Ted were a young Lena Horne. The black Hercules drifts his gaze down to Ted's exposed buttocks.

BIG MAN
Aww, Yeah!

The train slows to a stop. The teens guarding the opening doors with pistols in hand deny entry to those attempting to come aboard.

TEEN 1
This train is private! Wait for the next one!

The passengers back away. They get a partial view of Ted's situation. They gasp. The doors close.

Teen 3 nudges Teen 2 as they peek toward Ted and Big Man.

> **TEEN 3**
> Damn! That's nasty!

They hear Big Man's enjoyment mixed with Ted's muffled cries.

The train stops again. Like clockwork, the teens repeat their refusal of entry to the intended passengers. Big Man completes the act. As the doors begin to close, CP enters the violated passenger car. He hands Big Man a wad of money.

Money in hand, Big Man zips up his pants. The train begins to move.

Stretched out over the train seat, underwear and pants still down to his ankles, Ted is in tears and unable to look at anyone.

> **CP**
> Ted! You know these trains are not safe man! No telling who you're riding with.

CP looks at Ted, shaking his finger at Big Man.

> **CP**
> Twenty years in the joint can change your mind about what's sexy.

CP leans over to Ted's ear. He speaks softly.

> **CP**
> Ted, I'm not gonna kill ya. No more paydays to those punk-ass Disciples. You pay Loverstone.

CP stands straight so all can hear.

                              CP
            Now you remember that, and stop being a pain
            in the ass!

The Satan Lovers laugh. The train stops. On the platform, a dozen Satan Lovers are waiting for CP. The gangsters leave.

Ted is left alone to deal with staring train passengers.

INT NIGHT - Mrs. HELENA POWER'S bedroom

Mrs. P is on her knees at bedside.

                           MRS. P
            Dear God, protect my children from all hurt,
            harm, or danger. In Jesus's name, amen.

CAPTION: S/B SUPER:

FLASHBACK FALL 1960

EXT NIGHT - BRAGGS GROCERY STORE

A 1959 Oldsmobile pulls up and parks in front of a small neighborhood grocery store.

INT. OLDSMOBILE - NIGHT

Forty-three-year-old African American JAMES POWERS turns off the motor. He rubs the head of his ten-year-old son sitting next to him, CHARLES POWERS, nicknamed CP.

                        JAMES POWERS
            You're going to be as tall as me in a minute. You're
            growing fast, CP.

                           CP
I'm big enough to help out now. Huh, Daddy?

                    JAMES POWERS
C'mon, let's hurry up and get back home with that milk. You and your brothers drink it like water. You know how to find the milk in the store?

                           CP
Yeah, it's in the back, Daddy.

James and CP exit the car. They enter the store.

INT. NIGHT GROCERY STORE

CP speeds past the store counter manned by its black owner, WALTER BRAGGS, fifty-five, balding. James and Walter laugh at CP's enthusiasm.

                    WALTER BRAGGS
That boy sure is growing, Jim.

                    JAMES POWERS
Yeah, he's really taking on responsibility as a smart ten-year-old. He wants to help with everything.

                    WALTER BRAGGS
Well, at least he's not lazy. He's got that going for him.

The door opens. In walk two young black males, twenty-one years of age, with wide-brimmed hats, dark coats, and processed hairstyles.

                    WALTER BRAGGS
Get your son, Jim, and get out of here.

Pay me later for the milk.

Before James can respond, one of the young toughs slaps Walter. He then grabs Walter by the collar. They ignore James.

YOUNG GANGSTER 1
Your time's up, old man. You don't think you need protection? This is Chicago, man! You think Egyptian Cobras are jokin! Everybody needs protection over here.

James grabs Gangster 1 by the shoulders. He throws him back into Gangster 2. They both fall backward onto nearby stocked grocery shelves.

JAMES POWERS
Boy, are you out of your mind!

CP returns with the milk.

Gangster 2 gathers himself and stands, reaching under his coat.

He produces a pistol and points it at James.

YOUNG GANGSTER 1
Naw, old man, you the one who's got to be out of *they* mind!

Without hesitation, CP throws the bottle of milk at Gangster 1. The bottle hits its target. Gangster 1 drops his weapon due to the surprise strike. Walter quickly reaches under his counter for his waiting snub nose 38. Walter points and fires at Gangster 1. Gangster 1 falls.

James and Gangster 2 are now wrestling, attempting to grab the ⁿn pistol. The pistol is suddenly in young CP's reach, but he hesFor a brief moment, James's eyes meet CP's.

Walter cannot fire his weapon in fear of hitting James.

Just as CP decides to reach for the fallen 38 revolver, Gangster 2 wins the wrestling match.

CP rushes between Gangster 2 and his father, when simultaneously, Gangster 2 pulls the trigger. The gun misfires. James pushes his son away as the gun awakens. The slug hits James center chest. Simultaneously, Walter fires his pistol, killing Gangster 2.

>   CP
> Daddy!

CP reaches for his father who has fallen. CP's hands are covered in blood. The ten-year-old is traumatized.

>   CP
> Daddy! I'm sorry, Daddy. I'm sorry!

CAPTION: S/B SUPER: 1965

INT. BEDROOM - NIGHT

CP, now aged fifteen, awakens from this recurring dream, reliving the past, hoping for a different ending.

INT. OGDEN PARK GYM - FALL/NIGHT

Fifteen-year-old CP watches his schoolmates in sweat pants and knee pads compete. Mark wrestles BOBBY CHINA on a gym mat. Bobby China calls for a time out.

>   BOBBY CHINA
> Hold up. I learned "The Standing Switch" before
> y'all got here. Coach showed me.

CP
That's illegal, man.

MARK
You can't use that move in a wrestling meet!

CP
Naw, man, you could break a man's face doing that!

MARK
So!

CP
So, BOBBY CHINA, if you want to be disqualified and maybe in the Cook County Jail at fifteen, then you go ahead and do it!

BOBBY
I'm not talking about using it at a meet. I'm talking about *whoopin* somebody's ass. That's causing you a problem.

They stop wrestling. They stand up.

BOBBY CHINA
Okay, say you *humbugging* with somebody and he can't get passed your jab, so what does he do!

MARK
The punk grabs you and tries to wrestle.

BOBBY CHINA
Right, and when he does that, you do this!

Bobby China slowly goes through the *standing switch*, and Mark falls face first as Bobby China falls on top of him.

> MARK
> Damn!

> CP
> *Shoot*! Let me try it!

Bobby China practices the move with CP.

INT. GYM LOCKER ROOM - SAME NIGHT

The three friends are in the locker room getting dressed.

They wear Italian knits and pleated pants under long cashmere coats, topping it off with wide-brimmed hats, "*Gouster* style."

As the trio close their gym lockers and prepare to leave, Cp and Mark sing in two-part harmony.

> CP AND MARK
> Ooooo! La la La La! Oooo! La la La La!

> BOBBY CHINA
> Y'all hold on while I call Radio DJ Herb Kent The Cool Gent. Y'all ready for the radio? Happy birthday, Mark. See y'all.

Bobby China leaves.

> CP
> You're sixteen today huh?

MARK

Yeah, man, and I'm serious about getting into showbiz. Motown, man. Before I'm too old.

CP

Me too, man.

They leave the gym. They begin their walk home.

CP

I've always wanted to be in show business. I'm always standing in front of the mirror singing and stuff.

MARK

Me too.

Suddenly, shots are fired. Bullets bounce. They ricochet nearby. Everyone in range hits the ground. We hear shouting from the passing auto. Four passengers inside.

LARRY DAVEN

DISCIPLES!

The auto speeds away. The duo and the rest get to their feet.

CP

You saw who was in that car?

MARK

Naw, I wasn't looking.

CP

๊t dude from grammar school, Larry Daven, man! It seems like we ˙ting shot at every time a car crosses Racine and slows down!

> MARK
> Well, I sure ain't *turning* Disciple. I'll catch you at school tomorrow.
>
> Later, man!

(He runs off)

EXT. STREET - NIGHT

Mark is walking home. An auto passes him. The auto slows but then pulls away. Mark is startled but relieved. Mark, still a bit nervous, looks both ways as he crosses the empty street nearing his home. Suddenly, the auto reappears. It speeds toward him. Mark turns into a gangway between two apartment buildings. He runs blindly into the alley behind the buildings. He listens but hears nothing. He sees nothing when from behind he is struck with the butt of a pistol and goes down. A figure in the dark points a shotgun that peeks into the light.

> DISCIPLE ASSASSIN 1
> He's one of them, Satan Lovers. I think he's Richmond's brother.

EXT. APARTMENT BUILDING - NEXT DAY

CP leaves out of front door with schoolbooks under his arm.

His mother, Mrs. Powers, leans out of her front window.

> MRS. P
> Don't keep your girlfriend waiting.
>
> I don't want to hear her grandmother's mouth about you making her late for school.

                        CP

Okay, Ma!

CP meets his longtime girlfriend, BARBARA, at the corner of the street.

                     BARBARA

Let's go! We'll be late again!

                        CP

Not today! Your grandmother told us she's sending you back to your parents, cause I'm a bad influence.

Come on, let's run!

They jog briskly as CP takes her books.

                     BARBARA

Don't worry about that. My parents aren't interested in me, too involved with their MEDICAL careers. Did you watch the news this morning?

                        CP

Naw! I was running late.

                     BARBARA

One of those Satan Lovers got killed over the weekend.

                        CP

Satan Lovers! Can't be too many of them left. The Disciples are shooting at everybody.

                   BARBARA
    Well, I think if we go straight to school and stay
    off the streets at night, we should be alright.

                   CP
    Hey, you know I just want to make it to graduation and become a singing star, an actor, and marry you.

                   BARBARA
    I want that too, but when you become famous, you'll probably forget about me. (Jokingly)

                   CP
    Yeah, probably.

Suddenly an auto slows as it passes. It is not clear who is inside. CP notices a familiar feeling of concern encompassing him. Barbara doesn't pay the car any attention. The auto parks, and an elderly man exits.

                   CP
    But until then, I don't want to worry about us getting shot at every day either. (Looks at his watch) Dogg! It's almost 8:30, come on!

They begin double time to school.

INT. SCHOOL HOMEROOM - DAY

CP and Barbara hug and go separate ways. CP walks into his multicultural homeroom. Rabbit, a very short dark-skinned fifteen-year-old, sits next to CP. Bobby China, same age, tall dark-skinned youth with ice-cold slits for eyes, sits behind CP. Rabbit leans over to CP.

RABBIT
CP, what we goanna do!

CP
Do about what? What are you talking about!

RABBIT
You didn't see the news, man! Mark is dead! Ds killed him, man!

What Rabbit says does not sink in right away.

CP
Mark, what?

RABBIT
The NEWS said Ds killed Mark, man. What are we goanna do! He was one of us.

CP goes into a daze.

CP
Mark?! Naw, man!

BOBBY
I heard the Satan Lovers are having a meeting to deal with it tonight, 7:30, at the Sacred Heart Recreation Center.

Suddenly gun shots are fired outside school.

Disciples scream outside in a fast-moving car.

DISCIPLES
Disciples run it!

Some students duck under their seats, and the teacher is struggling to quiet other students who are angered, frightened, and screaming revenge.

TEACHER
Please, people, go back to your seats!

Please everyone calm down!

The teacher has lost control. Most students are very upset and angry, and some loudly file out of the classroom.

JOHNNY CALABRESE, a medium-build Italian fifteen-year-old, wearing jeans and a black leather jacket on top of a white T-shirt, goes to the window and peers out unafraid. His conversation with Barbara's friend Cynthia, aged fifteen, a dark-skinned beauty, has been interrupted by the shooting.

JOHNNY
JACK OFFS!

CYNTHIA
Be careful, John!

Cynthia ignores the look of disgust displayed by black and white students in earshot.

CP signals for his two friends. They head for the door. He speaks in monotone.

CP
Satan Lovers tonight, 7:30, at Sacred Heart.

Rabbit looks at Bobby. They are not sure how to respond.

                    BOBBY
Yeah, 7:30.

CP stops, turns to face the classroom, and addresses those students in front of him.

                    CP
Listen! If y'all tired of this and want to do something about it, you can! If you're tired of getting shot at by Disciples and scared to walk on the street, let's do something about it! Be at Sacred Heart Recreation Center tonight at 7:30! Satan Lovers are meeting tonight!
Come on! Be there! Tell everybody!

CP leaves the room followed by other classmates influenced by his words to spread the message.

INT. SCHOOL HALLWAY - DAY SAME.

The three friends go from student to student with the message. Other students follow their lead.

EXT. CHICAGO POLICE HEADQUARTERS - DAY

Police officers and civilians entering a large building with Chicago Police Headquarters atop the front entry.

INT. CHICAGO POLICE HEADQUARTERS MEETING ROOM - SAME DAY

Several plain-clothed members of the Gang Intelligence Unit (GIU) ˜eated in a small room receive instruction in a very private meeting ˥ its black chief officer Detective EDWARD Buchannon. About ˙rd are white and the rest black.

> OFFICER EDWARD BUCHANNON
> I've been informed that since we're a new unit in the department, nobody expects perfection right now. We're going to receive a little help from the Feds. Easy access into any district jail and all county jails to interview any Blackstone Ranger or Disciple. Now, I need everyone to be clear on what we're doing. Our job is to disrupt and terminate gang activity as we see it. But everything will be funneled through me and the commander only. Keep in mind those Rangers and Disciples we have a special interest in will be assigned judges who will cooperate with our needs.

Suddenly the closed door to the room opens, and OFFICER BUCHANNON is handed a note. He quickly glances at it.

> OFFICER EDWARD BUCHANNON
> All right, they confirmed it. The kid in Englewood who had his head blown off was connected to "The Satan Lovers" near our Englewood station. They're a smaller group we haven't heard much from lately.

One of the GIU members raises his hand. It's Officer Buchannon's partner, Detective Calvin Banks.

> OFFICER EDWARD BUCHANNON
> Detective.

> OFFICER CALVIN BANKS
> I got relatives in that area who say since this big White exodus, Negroes are moving farther west in Englewood, including Disciples. That's the reason for the recent and regular shootings out there. Negro population is nearly 68,000 between

Racine and Loomis near 63rd right now. Still growing. The only thing stopping the Disciples from adding to their numbers in west Englewood are those Satan Lovers.

OFFICER EDWARD BUCHANNON
Well, you know that's the Disciple mode of operation. They don't hold back on violence. Thanks, CALVIN. We better keep a closer eye out that way. But right now, our focus is east with the Rangers. They're more organized and growing. You all probably heard the Rangers are offering payoffs to police officers for photos of GIU Detectives?

The group mumbles with concern.

OFFICER EDWARD BUCHANNON
Our focus will start on those young Rangers in the county jail. Let's see how many are ready to talk and make a deal. Okay, you're dismissed.

The detectives close their notebooks and begin to exit the room.

OFFICER EDWARD BUCHANNON
(TO OFFICER BANKS)

Calvin. I think we should take a minute, drive through Englewood now, and check on your people. I got a hunch about that dead kid.

EXT. CP'S HOME - NIGHT

exits the front door of his mother's apartment building. CP goes he street. Rabbit and Bobby China are waiting.

> BOBBY CHINA
>
> Come on, man.

Without missing a beat.

> CP
>
> Let's go!

The three begin their walk to Sacred Heart Recreational Center with long strides in cadence as soldiers marching to war.

They hear someone shouting.

> LIL MANNY
>
> Hold up! We're going.

LIL MANNY, a short teenager who lost his left arm in a meat grinder accident, joins the trio with three of his friends.

> RABBIT
>
> C'mon, LIL MANNY! You part of this!

Rabbit hands Lil Manny a 25 automatic.

> RABBIT
>
> Hold this for me. That meat grinder took your arm, but not your heart, and you ain't got to worry about police.

As they pass, groups of 3, 4, 5, and more groups join ranks and include themselves on the trek to meet with the Satan Lovers street gang.

EXT. OGDEN PARK - NIGHT SAME

Detective Buchannon and his partner pull over. They park their unmarked police auto. They are amazed to see near two hundred young men with a number of females marching together, all high school age. The huge mass of youth approach 63rd Street into the stronghold of Six Tray Satan Lover territory. The group approach the Sacred Heart Catholic Church Recreational Center.

EXT. OUTSIDE SACRED HEART RECREATIONAL CENTER - NIGHT

Five foot, eleven inches tall and extremely dark-skinned, hard-core Satan Lover, ANDY is wearing a black jacket with the head of Satan and two pitchforks on the back. The head and pitchforks are encircled with the name 6-Tray (63rd Street) Satan Lovers. Andy is in a phone booth about to dial. He sees the massive body of enraged teens approaching. He hangs up. He automatically pulls a 32 revolver from his belt.

ANDY

DAMN!

Andy looks at the gun he's holding and then back to the approaching crowd. He quickly realizes the ineffectiveness of six bullets against the approaching mass of bodies. Andy returns the gun to his belt. He moves quickly into the building where Satan Lover leader and ex-boxer Richmond Williams with approximately 50 6-Tray Satan Lovers are discussing the Disciple problem. Richmond, approximately five feet and nine inches, with a menacing but confident demeanor, stands in front of the group with a serious temperament.

INT. SACRED HEART RECREATIONAL CENTER - NIGHT

dy enters the recreational hall, Richmond continues addressing nt. Well-dressed Satan Lover hierarchy, Alston WALKER,

Don Juan, SHORTY ROMAN, and Enforcer Joey Hilcomb stand next to Richmond.

> RICHMOND
> Royal Disciples caught Mark by himself. That's the last time we—

> ANDY
> Richmond! It's about a million dudes coming down Bishop Street!

Satan Lovers near Richmond pull weapons from their belts. Six feet, two inches tall, very black, muscle-bound Satan Lover, Joey Hilcomb raises his weapon and steps in front of Richmond. Other Satan Lovers post themselves near windows and doors and surround their leader.

(CALMLY)

> RICHMOND
> Hold up!

He walks past those guarding him and goes to the window. He takes a look.

> RICHMOND
> Andy, calm down. JOEY, put your piece away. Everybody, have a seat.

The group of Satan Lovers look at each other puzzled but follow instructions.

CP, Rabbit, and Bobby China enter the large room, which is quickly filled. Most of the crowd is unable to fit inside the recreation hall. Richmond appears unmovable. Richmond examines the young leaders in front of the angry mob. It is obvious. They are not Disciples.

                        CP
We brought some people to the meeting.

Richmond takes a beat. The crowd decreases its noise before he responds.

                     RICHMOND
What's your name, man?

                        CP
CP.

                     RICHMOND
Where you from?

                        CP
66th Street.

Richmond points to CP's companions.

                     RICHMOND
And where you from?

                    BOBBY CHINA
They call me Bobby China. I'm from 66th and Bishop.

                     RICHMOND
And you?

                      RABBIT
Rabbit, from Double 6.

Richmond addresses the crowd of angry teens.

RICHMOND
Everybody west of Racine, from now on, we are one family. The heads of Six Tray and "Double Six Satan Lovers" will be known as "The Family." From tonight on, we all together.

CROWD
Yeah! Right on! SATAN LOVERS!

RICHMOND
They took out Mark on his birthday! Now this is a NEW DAY! For Mark! You see how many here now! This is just the beginning. From now on, ah D step this side of Racine from 59th to 79th, he won't be a Devil's Disciple, 6 Tray Disciple, or Royal Disciple. He's gonna be a Dead Disciple!

Crowd goes wild.

RICHMOND
CP and his people from Double 6 gonna run everything from 66th to 79th. Business people are asking for help. Disciples come in and taking almost half of their weekly receipts and woopin' on old folks for just looking at 'em crooked. We're growing now!

SATAN LOVERS!

The chant passes back out into the crowd outside.

CROWD
SATAN LOVERS! SATAN LOVERS! SATAN LOVERS!

EXT. EMBROIDERY SHOP - DAY

CP and a dozen of his crew exit an embroidery shop with their newly purchased Satan Lover jackets.

EXT. COUNTRYSIDE WOODED AREA- DAY

Handsome, well-dressed Alston Flynn is loading a semi-automatic 12-gauge shotgun.

CP, Rabbit, and Bobby stood as observing students next to him.

> ALSTON
> You got to be able to shoot while you moving.
> That's the safest way not to get shot yourself.

Alston points at several cans with bottles lined up in front of him. Alston runs in front of the targets and fires his weapon as he passes, destroying them.

> CP
> You learn that in Vietnam, Alston?

> ALSTON
> Naw. My brother showed me. He was there. Ds took him out two years ago. Come on, Don Juan wants to show you something.

EXT. COUNTRYSIDE - DAY

We see Don Juan, Richmond's confidant, demonstrating to CP "the Quick Draw" from his belt.

EXT. COUNTRYSIDE - SAME DAY

Don Juan, always slickly dressed for the women, is holding a 38 and a 32 revolver. He places one pistol in his belt. Alston Walker stands beside him. CP and Bobby look on.

> DON JUAN
> Sometimes y'all got to work together, so you don't get caught out of ammunition. You stay behind cover, and one fires, as the other reloads. Like this.

Don Juan rapid fires the first weapon and passes it back to Alston, who begins reloading as Don pulls and fires the second weapon.

They again exchange guns when Don's second weapon is empty.

CP nods to Bobby. They exchange looks to acknowledge they both get the idea.

Don Juan hands a tall, very-dark-skinned sixteen-year-old lesbian, sporting a very short Afro, LINDA, leader of the female SL branch, The Satan Queens, an empty pistol.

He hands her shells. Linda begins to practice quick loading.

INT. MOTEL ROOM - NIGHT

CP with his main circle sit at a table with Don Juan in a motel room. Rabbit is inattentive, watching television. Don Juan is using a drawing, demonstrating the concept of "Triangular Assassination." Don Juan connects three dots surrounding the stick image of a person confirming that the assassins cannot miss. Bobby stares at Rabbit and abruptly turns off the television.

EXT. OGDEN PARK - DAY

CP on the top of a hill addressing fifty to sixty 66th Street Satan Lovers. He appears very animated as he provides strong instruction to the captains of his Satan Lovers branch.

EXT. 63RD STREET AND RACINE AVENUE, BORDERLINE BETWEEN THE SATAN LOVERS AND ROYAL DISCIPLES - NIGHT

SHORTY ROMAN RUSHEN whispers to CP standing in the shadows between two large apartment buildings with Rabbit.

> SHORTY ROMAN
> We used to do this back in the day to help enforce the Racine street borderline. Just to keep something on they mind. Hold on, check this.

Two teenagers wearing wide-brimmed hats with blue hat bands (a Disciple color) exit a nearby building. Shorty Roman jumps out of the darkness and begins to pistol whip one of the teens. CP and Rabbit punch the second and kick him as he scrambles to escape.

SHORTY ROMAN
Satan Lovers ain't going nowhere. This is Shorty Roman, punks! Lover Thang!

The Ds are allowed to run as Shorty Roman hands his pistol to CP.

SHORTY ROMAN
Here, man, do some damage.

CP takes the weapon. He is graduating in the ranks of gangsterdom. He fires a couple shots over the heads of the escaping Disciples. He, with the others, laughs and disappears back across Racine Ave.

EXT. 6 TRAY (63RD STREET) - NIGHT

It appears quiet in front of the Big Bear Liquor Store, Downtown, Satan Lover territory. Two teenagers exit the store and stop briefly to give the area alcoholic Dollar Man a quarter. Suddenly a slow moving auto with two Disciple assassins approach. One of the Ds begins to place his pistol out of the window in the direction of the store. CP and Rabbit exit the BEAR, when SHORTY ROMAN exits from the shadows. He runs across the front of the auto, firing a semi-auto 12-gauge shotgun named The Baby.

SHORTY ROMAN
Satan Lovers! Satan Lovers!

The front window of the auto caves in, and the vehicle takes off, swerving blindly down the street. The assassins escape without firing a shot. SHORTY ROMAN disappears in the darkness, laughing. CP realizes he is now a fifteen-year-old targeted professional gangster.

EXT. CLEANERS - DAY

CP is having a conversation with Bobby China and Shorty Roman Rushen waiting for Richmond in front of a dry cleaners on 63rd Street. Richmond exits.

> RICHMOND
> The owner said Ludo's been here and told him that Disciples are running everything around here now. I told him Ludo was a lie, but I don't think he believed me.

Richmond gets into his chauffeured auto and pulls away.

Shorty Roman signals to a car parked down the street. He shrugs his shoulders calmly speaking to CP and Bobby China.

> SHORTY ROMAN
> Sometimes we ain't got a choice.
>
> Disciples got some of these business owners really scared. So we got to be scarier. Some people are *hard* to help.

The auto drives by. It begins to fire through the front window of the dry cleaners. Shorty Roman stretches. He places his arms around CP's and Bobby China's shoulders. He continues to explain the Satan Lovers action as they slowly walk away.

INT. GROCERY STORE - DAY

Store owner LINCOLN is sweeping. Inside SL territory, two Royal Disciple leaders enter the store. Mean-looking twenty-one-year old

KILMAN, with MILLER, accompanied by one bodyguard, boldly approach Lincoln. The young bodyguard wears a Disciple jacket with the whole figure of the Devil on the back. Devils Disciples across the top. Kilman, a Disciple enforcer, is six feet and two inches tall, with a wide-brimmed hat. Miller, five feet and eleven inches, shows off his processed hair. Both well dressed.

> KILMAN
> Your name LINCOLN!

> LINCOLN
> Yeah, that's me.

Kilman looks around the store.

> KILMAN
> Today's payday.

> LINCOLN
> Hold on. I got it all ready for you. It's in the back. I'll get it.

Miller, "Black as night" processed hair, 185 pounds, is a Royal Disciples War chief.

> MILLER
> Kilman, you want a bottle of pop!

Miller signals a teen bodyguard to the cooler for the cold drink. Lincoln hesitates.

> MILLER
> What you waiting for, man!

> LINCOLN
> Yeah, I'll be right back.

Lincoln exits. Miller directs the armed Disciple to get the drink, when from the rear of the store Richmond enters making his presence known.

RICHMOND
Why are you bothering my people, Miller?

The armed Disciple starts to reach for his gun but stops after Miller signals him with his hand. Miller knows Richmond is not alone. Miller removes the bottle of pop held by his bodyguard and uses a bottle opener on the store counter to open it.

MILLER
Brother Richmond, what's happening?
What you need, some salami, cheese, and crackers? Hey, you change your mind? You turning your boys Disciple huh!

MILLER
Go back there, and get this brother what he needs.

CP enters behind Richmond. Two pistols held at his side.

CP
Don't *y'all* move.

MILLER
(CONDESENDING)
Damn, Richmond. I'm trying to be nice to you.
You don't run this no *mo,* man.

Richmond simply raises his hand. More than a dozen SLs fill the store entering from both entrances.

                    RICHMOND
I understand your point, Miller, but I'm thinking different on this.

The 2 Ds look at Miller for instruction.

                    RICHMOND
Tell your chief we got to respect each other better, cause if he sends anybody else over here messing with our people or our money, they not coming back. Tell your soldier to put his pistol on the floor.

Multiple Satan Lovers display their guns. Miller gives the order.

                    RICHMOND
Now go on, get outta here, cause y'all just don't know no better.

The Disciples exit smirking with confidence.

CAPTION: s/b SUPER: 1966 SPRING

EXT. BUILDING PORCH - DAY

CP is with his regulars in their usual Gouster dress. (Italian knits, pleated pants wingtips, and wide-brimmed hats). They approach Richmond and his chiefs sitting on or around the porch of a two-story apartment building. With Richmond's group are four Blackstone Rangers (with high bush haircuts). They wear black leather jackets with leather *cowboy fringe* on their sleeves and back. They have just concluded a conversation with Richmond.

The Rangers walk pass CP and crew.

                    BLACKSTONE RANGERS
Stone Love!

The RANGERS salute CP and his crew by rapping the left side of their chest with a right-hand fist.

RICHMOND
DOUBLE 6 SATAN LOVERS!

CP
What's happening, Richmond!

They do the African handshake. The rest partner up. They repeat the handshake.

RICHMOND
Glad to see you, my brother. Those are Blackstone Rangers. We're working together on this Disciple problem and other things. I want to talk to you, just me and you. Come on.

The duo signal for their brothers to stay, as they proceed to walk down a nearby alley. CP hands Richmond a bundle of money.

> RICHMOND
> I figure you about ready to handle picking up our money on the Tray.
>
> What you think?

> CP
> I think you know what's best Richmond. Everybody knows who's running this now, so it shouldn't be no problem.

> RICHMOND
> Naw, it shouldn't be. Listen, CP. Word got to me about what happened to your old man. They say there may be something more to what you're trying to do here.

> CP
> Don't know who you're talking to Richmond, but whatever happened to my old man and how I deal with it is my business. Those two Egyptian Cobras are dead and Mr. Braggs moved his family from Chicago right after.

Richmond examines CP.

> RICHMOND
> They say *they're* not sure who you're blaming, that you might have something against me even.

> CP
> I don't Richmond. Should I? There's not any more Egyptian Cobras like back then. Cobras

in the projects today, not really the same thing anyway.

RICHMOND
I hung around Cobras when I was younger, but, no you shouldn't CP? Those Ds ain't giving up no time soon. You heard about a brother called Sultan?

CP
Yeah, we heard of him. Ain't met him yet.

RICHMOND
You gonna meet him. When you do, he's gonna talk to you about some things. That's why I wanted to talk to you by yourself. To make sure you ain't got no other issues. Make sure you ain't got no problem working with him or me.

CP
I don't know him, Richmond. But as long as he ain't a Disciple, I got no problem working with him. I heard a lot of strong things about him.

RICHMOND
Yeah, he's been off the street for about a year and everything you heard is probably true, but he's back now and I want you to help him. He's gonna be my voice, and talking to him is like talking to me. You know what I mean?

CP
I know what you're saying.

RICHMOND
It's gonna get real crazy out here, CP.

> CP
> It's getting crazy out here no matter what I do.

> RICHMOND
> We can't let Disciples have this CP. If you're gonna stay in this, you're gonna have to do some things you never did before. You know what I mean!?

"Richmond sounds a bit more intense this time" You know what I mean!?

> CP
> I know what you mean.

> RICHMOND
> Everybody who's got a business this side of Racine is begging me to keep Ds from crossing over. They don't mind paying us because the Disciples will put them out of business sooner or later. Everybody else knows they're dead if they're not a Disciple in a D hood.

Richmond puts his hand on CP's shoulder.

> RICHMOND
> So things are gonna really be cold-blooded from here on. That's what Sultan's good at. We got to do what they do.

CP looks directly into Richmond's eyes.

> CP
> I can do whatever needs to be done, Richmond.

CHANGE IN TEMPO AND DEMEANOR

                RICHMOND
You know Martin Luther King Jr. is planning to march here in Chicago in August. No telling what's gonna happen with that. In Marquette Park too!

                CP
I respect Martin Luther King Jr., but he won't let anybody march with him who brings protection. That leaves us out.

The duo has stopped mid-alley when they hear LINDA accompanied by three tough-looking "sistas." The four girls wear black jackets decorated on the back with a horned, shapely female in red tights and pointed tail, encircled with "6 Tray Satan Queens." Linda yells loudly.

                LINDA
SATAN LOVERS! SATAN QUEENS!

                RICHMOND
LINDA! My sistah!

                LINDA
Sultan's out of jail. I saw him on the Tray.

EXT. MORNING SIDEWALK NEAR ENTRANCE TO HARPER HIGH SCHOOL. THE SCHOOL IS LOCATED WEST OF ASHLAND BLVD, THE DIVIDING LINE BETWEEN BLACK AND WHITE NEIGHBORHOODS – DAY

A group of white teens, including Johnny Calabrese, getting in their last cigarette puffs before entering school. They wear black jackets, with white T-Shirts and jeans. They are sons, nephews, and other family-related teenagers to mafia mob members. The young group is part of the Chicago generational Italian street gang called "The Hangouts." Their hairstyles resemble the likes of Elvis. They are listening to a loud transistor radio. We hear The Four Seasons sing "Sherry." (They have strong Chicago accents as with John Belushi, Dan Ackroyd, Joe Mantegna, etc.)

Their leader, Carlos Calabrese, gazes at the approaching group of black teens, which include CP. The black group appears to cater to CP.

> CARLOS
> All right Hangouts, here they come, moving into our neighborhood, into our schools, and into our families if we're not careful.

> BOBBY (a twin to Fabian)
> CARLOS, what do you mean our family?

> CARLOS
> I mean your sister, stupid. *Moolinyans* want to get to our sisters, asshole! They're like rabbits BOBBY, all they do is screw.

> BOBBY
> I heard the Martin Luther King Jr. guy is coming to town. Looks like they are trying to take over here.

> CARLOS
> Hey, I don't know. But my little brother over der, HE thinks it's okay. He loves these Moolies. Maybe he wants to be one. I don't know!

> JOHNNY
> Hey, don't start that again. My business is my business.

Bobby using his cigarette to point.

> BOBBY
> Who's the head Moolie der!

As the group of blacks get closer, CP looks at Johnny. Johnny stares at CP. They recognize they're in the same homeroom. CP nods his head in acknowledgment, so does Johnny. Carlos notices the exchange, but says nothing except

> CARLOS
> Who cares! As long as they keep their pistols pointed in the right direction. You know what I mean! Let's go.

The Hangouts throw down their cigarette butts and turn and file toward the school entrance.

As the crowd of black teens approach the school, before they enter, an unmarked police car pulls near the front of the crowd where CP and his crew lead. GIU officers Buchannon and Banks exit their vehicle after stopping it in the middle of the street. The officers, hands near their weapons, quickly approach CP.

> OFFICER EDWARD BUCHANNON
> So you all are Satan Lovers! We're officers with the Chicago Police Department GIU. Are you Charles Powers CP?

CP examines the two police officers, not knowing what their intention is. He turns and speaks to his followers, responding calmly.

> CP
>
> Gang Intelligence Unit.

CP returns his attention to Officer Buchannon.

> CP
>
> Yeah, that's me.

Buchannon invades more space, slowly stepping toward CP staring. CP returns the stare. They are almost nose to nose.

> OFFICER BUCHANNON
>
> We just wanted to introduce ourselves to a new chief in the Satan Lovers.

Officer Buchannon hands CP a business card.

> OFFICER EDWARD BUCHANNON
>
> Here's my card. I want you to call me if you think we can help with your Disciple problem out here. We want to do what we can, so no more kids get killed over here for nothing.

CP does not respond.

> OFFICER EDWARD BUCHANNON
>
> Most important thing is we want you to know that we know who you are and that we'll be watching you, CP.

> RABBIT
>
> How come *y'all ain't* watching those white boys!

> OFFICER EDWARD BUCHANNON
>
> They're not killing each other, punk! Are they?

The detectives head back to their car.

> OFFICER EDWARD BUCHANNON
> You stay in touch here, and don't be late for school.

The officers drive away.

The group finally enters the school.

INT. SAINT BRENDAN'S CATHOLIC SCHOOL GYMNASIUM DANCE FLOOR - NIGHT

CP and his main boys are greeted by Joey Hilcomb and several Satan Lovers waiting in front of Saint Brendan's school gymnasium. R&B music can be heard coming from the inside. CP notices his girlfriend, Barbara, standing against the wall, arms folded, looking at him scornfully. He approaches her.

> BARBARA
> Where's your girlfriend? I know you don't come to these dances by yourself.

CP is very surprised to see Barbara who is not a regular.

> CP
> What are you doing here?

> BARBARA
> Well, since you don't spend much time with me at school anymore or church, I heard about this. I figured if I showed up here, at least I'd get a better idea of what's going on.

> CP
> What do you mean what's going on?

BARBARA
How come you didn't invite me to come with you?

CP
Barbara, this really is no place for you.

BARBARA
Why? If it's a place for you, why is it not a place for me?

CP
There's a lot happening with me now, Barbara. I know I'm not getting with you like I used to but it's not because I don't think about you.

BARBARA
Well, I can't read your mind, Charles, I can only see what you do and don't do. I heard they have this Set every Friday. Just tell me you don't want to—

Suddenly, there's commotion and shouting. A fight has broken out. Joey has smacked one of three Ds now fighting their way to the front door. CP points to a safe corner.

CP
Stand over there, okay?

Barbara nervously follows instructions. CP calls for two nearby SLs to guard her. The escaping Disciples run past CP.

CP
They'll keep an eye on you.

CP signals for Rabbit.

> CP
>
> Do me a favor, man. Make sure she gets home. She lives right on 64th. That's my girl. Be careful.

> RABBIT
>
> All right, man. I'll take her. Be right back.

The crowd is moving toward the door onto the street. Joey Hilcomb, with several SLs, examines each person passing, looking for more Ds as the others have escaped. CP joins the group standing outside the front entrance when suddenly a car turns the corner with the escaped Disciples.

> DISCIPLES IN CAR
>
> Punk-ass Satan Lovers! We'll be back! Disciples run it!

Joey quickly pulls his 38 and fires toward the car. CP walks directly into the path of gunfire and ducks.

Joey continues, pulling the trigger and totally oblivious to what happened to CP.

> JOEY
>
> Satan Lovers!

Barbara, with her escort, gets into a car. Barbara watches.

CP looks at Barbara. Their eyes meet. She sees everything.

> BARBARA
>
> Rabbit? What's all this about? Why is everyone shooting at each other? I really don't understand.

Rabbit instructs Barbara to get into the car.

> RABBIT
> Barbara, CP asked me to get you home, not to explain something I don't even understand myself.

Barbara wants an answer before she gets into the car.

> BARBARA
> Are you serious? You're involved in this and don't know why?

> RABBIT
> What I know is if I get shot at, I duck and shoot back! Now get in the car. Okay! 64th Street, right?

Barbara reluctantly nods yes. She gets into the car, unsatisfied with Rabbit's answer. They drive off. CP watches them leave.

CP leaves the crowd of Satan Lovers and walks alone to the stairs in front of a single-story home. He sits on the stairs in deep thought. He understands he missed his demise from a friend by inches. This isn't the life or death he had foreseen for himself. He has always viewed his future as a Hollywood entertainer.

> CP
> Man! Damn! Damn!

EXT. 63RD STREET (6 TRAY) - NEXT NIGHT

CP and his two main boys are waiting outside of the Big Bear liquor store.

INT. BIG BEAR LIQUOR STORE - NIGHT

Dollar Man, black, approximately sixty-five, shabby-looking wine head, is standing at the store counter when the cashier places a fifth of Wild Irish Rose in a bag. He hands it to him.

>   CASHIER
> Listen, remind CP that I appreciate him doing it this way. I'll be in big trouble selling it to teenagers.

>   DOLLAR MAN
> Yeah, yeah, he knows all that!

EXT. BIG BEAR LIQUOR STORE - SAME NIGHT

Dollar Man exits the store with the bag of Wild Irish Rose wine. The wine head hands over the bag to Bobby China. Rabbit hands Dollar Man a few bills. CP and his close friends walk around the corner under the EL Tracks into an alley.

EXT. ALLEY - SAME NIGHT

Bobby China pours out a portion of wine.

>   BOBBY CHINA
> For those brothers not here anymore.

They pass the Brick of Rose around the group. They all drink their portion.

>   CP
> I don't know why we're always drinking this Rose. We can afford better.

                          RABBIT
Hey, we been doing this since we started high school. It's our thang.

                           CP
Okay, so when we graduate from school, we graduate from Rose, cool?

They all laugh.

                          RABBIT
Okay, man.

                           CP
Heard on the news about those Blackstone Rangers coming down on those East Side Disciples?

                          RABBIT
I seen 'em on TV singing and thangs with Oscar Brown Jr. You know Clifton at school? He's a Blackstone Ranger. He wears his jacket and everything.

                           CP
Sure he can. Cause Disciple's in check out this way. Those Rangers were on TV singing, huh? If I live through this, I'm still gonna be a singer. Pass that Rose.

CP takes a hit.

                           CP
I'm gonna get to Hollywood one day.

CP's companions give a "Sure you will" look at each other, but do not dare burst CP's bubble. Rabbit reaches for the bottle. He takes a long swig. Bobby China changes the subject, staring at Rabbit hogging the Rose.

BOBBY CHINA

What! You just gonna kill the wine, Rabbit! Ain't our fault you ain't got no girlfriend. You can't drink that out your mind, man!

RABBIT

I rather do without a girlfriend if I had to deal with that skinny drink of water you got. She looks like six o'clock, straight up and down.

BOBBY CHINA

Hey, if you weren't a midget, I wouldn't let you get away with that. Trying to hog *all* the wine and drink your troubles away.

CP

Hey, man, Rabbit had a fine girlfriend back in the day. You remember Shirley Johnson in the sixth grade!

BOBBY CHINA

That don't count. We were *all* the same size back then.

CP

I remember when the church took us all on that hayride out in the country. We were all talking about what we wanted to be when we grew up. Everybody was with their little girlfriend.

> BOBBY CHINA
> That's right. We were on that hay wagon with the horses. That was the first time I'd ever seen real horses.

> RABBIT
> Come to think of it, CP was with the same girlfriend he got now. That's the same Barbara, right?

CP takes a beat and then reaches for the bottle of Rose.

INT. HORIZON LOUNGE - SAME NIGHT

A den of Royal Disciples meets inside the Horizon Lounge, five blocks east of the Satan Lover Disciple boarder, temporarily closed to the public.

Devil Disciple chief Ludo speaks intently to the group of approximately 30 Royal Disciples gathered around the room. He is ending his presentation.

> LUDO
> David told me himself. All we got to do is keep those punk-ass Satan Lovers in check.

> MILLER
> Scaring those punks is one thing, but somebody gotta come up with a murder beef sooner or later.

His eyes search the room.

> LUDO
> Miller, can't nobody catch a beef if nobody knows who's doing what. -You know what I'm saying, Miller?

> MILLER
> Ludo, I heard Sultan was back. They got a bunch of new Satan Lovers run by a dude named CP. Him and Richmond set us up when me and Kilman were over there collecting. Richmond said any Disciple trying to collect in the hood is dead.

> LUDO
> You scared? Y'all gonna be bigger than Eastside. So get ready to get rich. See y'all later. D THANG!

The thugs mingle as they depart. Ludo puts his arms around two shadowed figures who have spoken to no one, lingering in the shadowed rear of the lounge.

EXT. STREET OUTSIDE HORIZON LOUNGE - NIGHT

Ludo and his driver exit the lounge. They enter an auto, which has pulled up near the entrance. Parked in their unmarked police vehicle across the street from the Disciple meeting are GIU detectives Buchannon and Banks.

INT. UNMARKED POLICE CAR - NIGHT

> OFFICER EDWARD BUCHANNON
> He's coming out now. Yeah, there's no doubt. If Ludo's over here, there's something big happening on this side of State Street.

> OFFICER BANKS
> Yeah, that's what I've been thinking, and if it's happening this side of Halsted Street, it's going to involve the Satan Lovers.

OFFICER EDWARD BUCHANNON
We're going to need more manpower over here and might as well set that up sooner than later.

OFFICER BANKS
Why's that?

OFFICER EDWARD BUCHANNON
Think about it, Calvin. If Ludo's taking time to meet with these Royal Disciples, that means their King is placing a significant amount of focus out this way. Even at the same time, he's dealing with those Rangers out East.

OFFICER BANKS
Yeah, so what, he's got enough people to do that. The Satan Lovers can't match The Disciples in numbers.

OFFICER EDWARD BUCHANNON
That's the point. Just because of that reason, you can believe that The Satan Lovers will be uniting with the Rangers, just like The Four Corners, The Vicelords, and The Cobras. Yeah, I think things are gonna get hotter on the West side of Englewood.

EXT. BIG BEAR LIQUOR STORE - SAME NIGHT

6 Tray Satan Lovers KENT and WILLIAM, wearing their Satan Lover jackets, exit the Big Bear Liquor Store. They obtain their Rose from Dollar Man out front. They head for the alley.

Kent is a short stout teen, approximately fifteen.

                          KENT
         Pretty soon we won't need no cop, man, and old
         Dollar Man is gonna be out of a job.

WILLIAM, TALL AND SLIM, AGED FIFTEEN.

                        WILLIAM
         Yeah, Richmond says we gonna be running
         things past Ashland Avenue on the White side
         pretty soon. He said we gonna own the Big Bear
         straight out.

EXT. DARK ALLEY - NIGHT

Kent sees CP with his boys approaching as they pass through a beam of track light showering between El train tracks above.

                          KENT
         CP! Double 6 Satan Lovers!

         What's happening!

Now walking into near total darkness under the tracks and trains.

                           CP
         What's going on, young brothers!

         Y'all 6 Tray, right?

                          KENT
         Yeah. We just come back here to kill this brick.

Bobby China tosses his empty bottle of Rose to the litter filled dirt floor. William holds up the bag containing his wine. He turns the bottle of Wild Irish Rose upside down, slaps the bottom, and turns it over. He cracks the cap. He brings the bottle to his mouth.

CP
Hold up, young brother. What you gonna do?

WILLIAM
Yeah, you're right.

He begins to pour out a portion of wine.

CP
There ya go. Give our boy Mark a hit.

William gives CP the Black handshake and then a manly hug. He then takes a sip.

WILLIAM
Heard about him.

CP
How long y'all been Satan Lovers?

WILLIAM
Since about eleven. Both of us. I'm WILLIAM, and this is KENT. We're fifteen now. Linda's my sister. She runs the Satan Queens.

Bobby China attempts to fight off the effect from the alcohol and straightens up.

BOBBY CHINA
We met your sister, man. She's a hard girl.

William takes a hit of wine and offers it to CP.

WILLIAM
Want a hit?

Bobby China reaches for the bottle when out of nowhere there are loud voices. Flashes from gunfire. The flashes illuminate two shadowy figures.

                FIGURES IN THE DARK
Disciples punk!

                          CP
Move!

All the Satan Lovers attempt to take cover. There is no time to return fire. The shadows fire at CP but miss, ricocheting off an El pillar.

Bobby China and Rabbit have found cover behind an El pillar. They drunkenly fumble at retrieving their weapons. The firing guns refocus on another target. William has no chance.

He's hit several times. He is spun around and held up by the bullets entering his body. The Rose crashes to the ground.

                        KENT
Wil—

Kent moves toward William and catches a slug to the leg.

He falls. The two figures run up to the crawling boys.

                        KENT
Damn Viet Cong ass D's! Satan Lovers Punks!

Kent's body is thrown around as multiple shells mangle his limp frame. We cannot see the faces of the two-man kill team. They duck the now-returned fire by Bobby China and Rabbit. They trot back and totally disappear into the darkness pursued by the two Satan Lovers. CP has returned to William's side. He confirms that he is not breathing. He also examines a deceased Kent. CP's face is suddenly hardened with determined vengeance. Shadows run down the dark alley.

> DISCIPLE 1
> Hear what they still calling us?
> Viet Cong!! Ain't that a bitch!

EXT. CHURCH FUNERAL - DAY

The service has ended, as the Pastor steps toward the parents and family members. The song "Open Our Eyes" assists him in comforting family. The attendees begin to stand and begin the procession viewing the two bodies placed in flower-covered caskets as it exited the church.

Two Satan Lovers, in all black, wearing a red armband, stand at attention to the left and right of two coffins. They show no emotion. The viewing is nearing its end. CP, Don Juan, Alston, Li'l Manny, Bobby China, and Rabbit, are followed by four uniformed Blackstone Rangers (who wear all black with a green stripe down each pant leg, their Blackstone emblem Pyramid posted to the left of their suit jackets) viewing the bodies. A host of Satan Queens, also in black with red berets, pass and bow to Linda and family members, as they begin their exit from the church. A host of Satan Lover soldiers stand on each side of the church entrance, wearing black wide-brimmed hats and red hat band. Most wearing black leather or long black cashmere coats.

Richmond in all black with a red tie, followed by CP, their close Satan Lover Chieftains, and Stones are the last to exit the church. Dozens of civilians and Satan Lovers have already filed past the statuesque guards.

Walking toward the Satan Lovers exiting the church, wearing all black, wide-brimmed hat, black leather coat, and gloves, is SULTAN. He is approximately six feet, two hundred pounds, with two pearl handled 357 caliber pistols positioned in his belt, clearly visible up close. A Satan Lover since aged twelve, recently released from juvenile incarceration, his goal in life is to insure the life span of the Satan Lovers, single-handed if necessary. He stops.

He faces the approaching group.

       RICHMOND
  CP, this is SULTAN. Y'all walk me to my car.

Sultan and CP shake hands. They escort Richmond to his chauffeured Cadillac.

       RICHMOND
  I want y'all to figure out how you gonna handle
  what happened to these boys. Find out who these
  Viet Cong punks are and take 'em out. It's two
  of 'em right?

       SULTAN
  Yeah, police said two.

       CP
  They live in our hood somewhere close. When
  they hat up, nobody ever sees them hop in a ride.
  Without a car, they disappeared too fast at night
  not to know the area.

       SULTAN
  But there getting too bold. They're gonna slip
  and have no place to run one day.

       CP
  Man! You're right! That's where they're weak.
  Every time they come out of nowhere and pop
  at us, everybody scatters and runs. They've been

using revolvers, which means they only got twelve shots.

RICHMOND
What you getting at?

CP
The only time our people get hit is when they're right on top of them, say a yard or less. Any further than that, they can't hit a damn thing.

RICHMOND
So what?

SULTAN
(He gets it)
So if Satan Lovers don't run, stay out of range till they empty their pistols, and you got two dead Disciples.

CP
They didn't think that possibility through. I know they didn't.

RICHMOND
And you *hope* they only got two pistols.

CP
Yeah, it's a gamble, but a *good* one.
We got to put an end to this!

Richmond gets into chauffeured Cadillac Seville.

SULTAN
We'll pass the word. Next time Viet Cong pop out, nobody runs!

>   RICHMOND
> See you at the cemetery.

The car drives off.

Across the street, half a block down in an unmarked police car are Detectives Buchannon and Banks.

>   BANKS
> Yeah, I saw the Stones, but who we gonna follow? We going to the cemetery or the Eastside?
> (In deep thought)

>   BUCHANNON
> Back to the station.

INT. CP'S HOME - DAYS LATER NIGHT

CP with his two brothers finish dinner. Mrs. P is washing dishes. CP pushes back his plate, ready to leave the table. His two younger brothers, EDDIE and RANDOLPH, continue to eat at the table. Mrs. P is washing the dishes.

>   RANDOLPH
>   (CURIOUS, FIDGETY)
> CP, are you a Gouster or a Collegian?

>   CP
> Don't you see these pleats and these kicks, RANDOLPH? These are comforts I got on. I don't dress like a punk Collegian.

>   RANDOLPH
> You a Gouster, huh? I want to be a Gouster, too.

> **CP**
> Cool. You gonna be thirteen this year.

It's about that time.

> **MRS. P**
> Collegian means going to college, right? I don't like that Gouster stuff. You look more like gangsters instead of someone thinking about college. Now that's where your brothers are going.

Eddie continues to eat, with no response.

> **MRS. P**
> Isn't that right, Eddie??

Eddie doesn't look up but nods yes.

> **MRS. P**
> He's only fourteen, but he knows how to stay out of trouble and away from the wrong type of people.

CP slowly gets up from the table and readies to leave the home. He believes his mother's statement is a dig. *It is.*

> **MRS. P**
> CP, I need you to keep your *tail* at home tonight. You're staying out later, and later it seems like. You need to spend some time at home.

> **CP**
> I can't miss wrestling practice tonight, Ma.

MRS. P

You really need to stop lying. I can't remember the last time you went to some practice. You're still a child—

CP
(Interjects quickly)

I'm sixteen!

MRS. P

And sixteen isn't grown! I'm tired of you lying and coming in after ten o'clock like you don't have any sense! I *said* keep your *tail* in tonight, and I mean it!

CP's brothers, Randolph and Eddie, are waiting for a response.

Mrs. P stands ready to fight. CP bends down and finishes the small amount of food remaining on his plate, and he stands. He begins to grab his cashmere coat. Mrs. P snatches the coat. CP can't be punked, even by his mother.

CP

Momma, give me my coat. I'm not going to put my hands on you.

MRS. P

You say you what! You're not going to do what!

Mrs. P throws the coat at him.

MRS. P

Here's your coat, and let me get the rest of your things. You don't want to put your hands on me! You done lost your mind!

CP

Yeah, you right, Momma. It's time for me to go somewhere else. I ain't no baby no more.

Mrs. P goes into CP's bedroom and quickly returns with a few articles of clothing in a shopping bag. She throws them at CP.

MRS. P

Boy, you better go somewhere before I kill you. I know about you and your gangster friends. You go ahead and let them take care of you. You're not going to stay in this house and even think about putting your hands on me!

CP picks up the shopping bag and begins his exit from home.

MRS. P

And I'm not going to let you have your brothers thinking it's okay. Your Satan Lovers and Devil's Disciples are following the same leader. The Devil and Satan are the same person! I'm still praying for you, but you got to get out of here until you see that!

CP leaves without responding. Eddie gets up from the table to follow CP. Mrs. P has gone to her bedroom.

CP drops his bag before reaching the front door, and Eddie picks it up.

EDDIE

Everybody knows you a leader in the Satan Lovers now. A lot of people at church know too. They told Ma. A lot of people telling Ma that someone is gonna come by and shoot through our windows one night, and she's scared.

                    CP
        Come here, EDDIE. Look there.

CP opens the front door and points at two Satan Lovers sitting in a parked car in front of their home.

                    CP
        Hardly anybody knows about this address, but we got somebody watching all the time, just in case.

                    EDDIE
        Where you going? You gonna be all right, man?

                    CP
        Yeah, man, I'm all right. I'm gonna have somebody give you money at school for Ma every once in a while. This wasn't working out anyway. I've got more than three hundred soldiers under me. What does it look like for me to have to be in the house by ten o'clock! Look out for our little brother.

CP retrieves a pistol covered near the door entrance and places it under his belt. They hug.

                    CP
        Later, man.

                    EDDIE
        Okay, see you later.

CP exits. He signals for the parked guards to remain in place. CP walks toward 63rd Street.

EXT. 63RD STREET - SAME NIGHT

CP walks into a phone booth on the Tray. He readjusts the revolver in his belt and dials.

EXT. STREET SIDEWALK - DAY

Among the many Black students crossing Ashland into the white-only neighborhood surrounding Harper High School are CP and his two main associates surrounded by Satan Lover soldiers.

They note in an alley a group of five black youth like a wolf pack surrounding a white youth wearing a black leather jacket.

>CP
>(To Rabbit)
>Hold up. Let me check this out. Rest of *y'all* go on ahead.

As CP approaches, to his surprise, it's Johnny Calabrese defending his leather jacket with a 2×4.

>BLACK YOUTH 1
>Give it up, Gray boy. Don't make us take that coat off you.

>BLACK YOUTH 2
>You ain't got no business this close to Ashland anyway. You messing with one of our sisters too! We should kick your ass just for that!

>JOHNNY
>Sure, you Jack Off! You want it? Take it! All of yous, c'mon!

CP removes his coat, hands it to Rabbit, and positions himself back to back with Johnny.

> CP
> It takes five of *y'all* against one!
> It's two of us now. Now what!

The black wolf pack recognizes CP.

> BLACK YOUTH 1
> What you doing CP? That's a gray boy, man! He's messing with a sister too!

> CP
> I don't care what he is! He's by himself. Poot Butts! Five jumping on one. If he got heart enough to be this close to Ashland by himself, you respect his heart, if nothing else!

> BLACK YOUTH 1
> Yeah, we hear you, man. We outta Here. Satan Lover thang, man.

> JOHNNY
> Hold it! (He shouts.)
> Where you going!

Johnny whacks the black youth on the ankles with his 2×4.

> JOHNNY
> I want that watch you wearing, Piss Wipe!

CP to black youth on ground wreathing in pain.

> CP
> You heard what he said. Give him the watch, man.

Rabbit hands CP his coat and removes the watch from the youth's wrist.

> RABBIT
> We not taking nothing from you.
> It's a gift, right?!

The remaining four black youth pick up their friend.

> BLACK YOUTH 1
> Yeah, man. Damn!

Rabbit tosses the watch to CP. Rabbit puts his arm around the fallen youth. He assists him up.

> CP
> Catch you later, Rabbit.

As Rabbit and the wolf pack leave, CP hands the watch to Johnny.

> JOHNNY
> Keep it.

Johnny walks to school in silence.

INT. SCHOOL SAME DAY

CP retrieves books from his school locker. Rabbit waits. CP looks up. CP sees Barbara approaching, appearing sexy but serious. Rabbit reads the situation.

                          RABBIT
I'll see you in class, CP.

RABBIT EXITS.

                         BARBARA
So where do you live now?

CP props a pencil above his ear. He ignores her question.

                           CP
How you doing? Late for class huh?

                         BARBARA
So where do you live now?

                           CP
What do you mean?

BARBARA

CP, I know almost everything. I saw you nearly shot and killed by your gangster friends. I know you don't live with your mother anymore. I know you're some kind of leader in the Satan Lovers, but what I *don't really* know is how you feel about me.

CP

We better get in class. We're already late.

BARBARA

Our classes aren't going anywhere. They'll be here, but I'm not sure if you will. You've made a lot of decisions about your life without me. You have really changed. No more Hollywood dreams? Don't I count anymore, Charles?

CP looks at Barbara intently.

CP

I love you, Barbara. I always have, always will.

BARBARA

If we love each other and plan for a future together, shouldn't we make important decisions together!

CP

I don't see myself as a gangster. We're under attack in the neighborhood. People need help. Yeah. I decided on my own that I can and will do everything to protect my neighborhood.

BARBARA

Charles, all I want is—

                            CP
             Barbara let's talk later. Here.

CP takes the pencil from his ear. He writes something on Barbara's notebook. He takes her hand gently and kisses it, looking lovingly into her eyes.

                            CP
        Meet me at this address right after school.

CP turns. He walks down the hall to his homeroom class.

Barbara reads the address CP has written on her notebook.

EXT. BOBBY's MOTEL - NIGHT

Barbara walks toward the entrance of Robert's Motel. She checks the address again. She enters. Barbara notes an elderly gentleman behind a desk. Alston Walker is standing near the desk, talking with SL enforcer Joey Hilcomb. They are counting receipts when they notice her enter.

                           JOEY
                       (TO BARBARA)

            Just a minute. Have a seat, mam.

He picks up the DESK phone and dials.

                           JOEY
             She's here.

A car suddenly pulls up. Rabbit and Bobby China exit the car with two Satan Lover soldiers. They enter the motel. Rabbit sees Barbara and gives a questioning look to Joey. Joey nods to Rabbit.

                            RABBIT
              Hey, Barbara. CP'll be here in a minute.

Joey Hilcomb bags the receipts and gives one package to Alston.

They exit with Rabbit and Bobby China. They get into the car. It pulls off. The remaining two Satan Lover soldiers have a seat in the lobby. The older desk clerk continues his program when CP appears. Barbara is stunned by all the activity she has just witnessed.

                              CP
                         (TO BARBARA)

Come with me this way.

CP leads his queen into a makeshift luxury suite, with flowers, wine, etc.

                            BARBARA
              This is beautiful! Is that wine?

                              CP
              I have more friends now.

CP grabs Barbara tenderly, closer to his body.

                              CP
              I'm sorry. It's been so long since we've been alone.

CP's no longer a kid. He kisses his love interest incessantly. They fondle each other. Heat and passion are in the air.

CP removes his shirt, and they continue. Moments later, CP attempts to remove Barbara's blouse. She initially appears to cooperate but then pulls back. She appears to feel guilty.

BARBARA
CP, I can't.

CP continues. She can't be serious.

BARBARA
CP, I said I can't. Not yet. All this is really nice, but I said I can't. You've grown up pretty fast, CP. Maybe too fast. I haven't!

CP
Barbara, you said you know all about everything. So you have an idea how I got this room, all of this. You said you weren't sure how I feel about you. I'm just trying to show you.

BARBARA
Charles, knowing what you want and being ready for it are two different things. I'm only sixteen. I'm still a kid. I don't drink wine. You're living in a world ahead of where I am now. I need you to be that Hollywood singer and actor accomplishing your dream. I didn't realize that until just now.

She's ready to leave.

BARBARA
I'll see you in school, if you continue to come.

Barbara gathers herself. She gently pulls back and looks into CP's eyes for understanding. She receives it, turns, and exits the room. Satan Queen leader, Linda, exits an adjacent door with two cute female gangsters. Barbara and Linda's eyes make brief contact. Barbara hesitates but continues her exit. Linda and her sexy staff cross the hall. They knock on CP's closed door.

INT. PIZZERIA - DAY

Calabrese Pizza Place/Pool Room, Bar. Hangout of the Italian Street Gang. Seated in a booth are the owner Mafia Chieftan Emilio Calabrese and his nephew, Caesar Cavouti, with Emilio's oldest son Carlos. Young Johnny Calabrese joins them with two "made" mafia men, GLASSES and SHOES GARIBALDI. Johnny grabs a seat. He disobediently reads a *Jet* magazine pulled from his jacket. Caesar happens to look in Johnny's direction.

          CAESAR
Li'l John, I *gotta* tell 'em. So don't get upset.

To the group

          CAESAR
So listen, we're in my car. He asked me to drop him off at school. On the way, I say to 'em, "Since you love these Moolies so much, why don't you walk to school with dem!" I'm **just** yanking his Johnson Ya know. The kid says, "Pull over!"

Caesar ruffles Johnny's hair. Johnny doesn't like it.

          CAESAR
GLASSES, the kid's got Yams! The kid grabs the door handle and says, "Let me out!"

          GLASSES
Hold it! So you drive the kid to Ashland and let 'em walk!

          CAESAR
Glasses, I pull over, and he gets out on his own!

SHOES
But he's got a piece right?

CAESAR
SHOES! That's what I'm sayin! I tries to give 'em a little 25 auto just in case. I figure we don't want ta wack any kids, even if der are Moolies. He won't take it! And here dey come a whole street full of Moolies. The kid slams da door and walks right at 'em. He freakin' disappears in the crowd of Moolies! They turn the corner, and he's gone!

SHOES
Then what'd you do Caesar?

CARLOS
What do you think he did! He calls my Old Man and says "UNCK, cousin Johnny's dead!" *Please don't whack me!*

Emilio Smiles. Shoes cracks up laughing.

CAESAR
I drives around the block and don't see 'em. I says a little prayer to's Saint Christopher. I goes to the school, uncle Emilio and Carly tells me the kid's in his class without a scratch.

CARLOS
Lucky yous! And drop the Carly, I told ya!

Thick Italian accent.

GLASSES
Li'l John, what was yousa thinkin! Thosea spooks coulda killed ya, witda no piece or nutin!

Emilio hands Johnny a slice of pizza and pats his son's hand. Thick Italian Accent. Sixty-eight plus salt-and-pepper hair

>   EMILIO
>   He's a lota like his olda man. Just a little crazy
>   and don't takeah no ah shit offa of nobody.

Emilio signals for Carlos and whispers in his ear. Carlos signals Caesar to follow him. He exits the hangout. Caesar follows him cautiously. Glasses cleans his large eye wear.

>   GLASSES
>   You're a gooda boy, John.

Johnny has not spoken a word. He moves to the pool table, with pizza wedged in his jaw, and removes a pool stick from a Hangout about to take an important shot. Johnny takes it and continues the game. He devours the pizza awarded him by his dad.

EXT. BOBBY's MOTEL - AUGUST NIGHT

Several Satan Lovers standing in front of their makeshift headquarters, BOBBY's Motel. They are in relaxed conversation.

INT. BOBBY's MOTEL - NIGHT SAME

CP is reading a schoolbook, while Bobby China is eating Chinese food and cleaning his weapon. Rabbit watches the TV News when…

>   RABBIT
>   CP, check this out!

On television is the infamous news footage of Martin Luther King Jr. and his march through Chicago's Marquette Park. In the crowd of name-calling whites tossing rocks is the brother of Johnny Calabrese and Hangout leader, Carlos, in addition to other Hangout and white Harper High School students.

> NEWS MAN
> On this historic date of Friday August 5, 1966, Martin Luther King decided to take his protest to Chicago's South side. Struck on the head by a rock thrown by a group of hecklers, Dr. Martin Luther King falls to one knee. Dr. King regained his feet and led a group of marchers, demonstrating alleged housing discrimination through an all-white district in Chicago. Marching into the all-white housing areas near Marquette Park, the protesters had bottles, bricks, and rocks thrown at them.
>
> They courageously continued with the march...

> RABBIT
> Ain't that Calabrese!

Gulping down Chinese food.

> BOBBY CHINA
> Ain't *that* some mess!

NEWS FOOTAGE CONTINUES

> NEWS MAN
> This incident at Marquette Park is part of the protests led by the Chicago Freedom Movement, of which King is co-chairman. This is part of a year-long campaign for open housing.

INT. SCHOOL

Caption: s/b Super: Monday, August 8, 1966, day
School cafeteria, lunchtime
CP, with a small entourage of followers, enters the school lunch line. The lunchroom is moderately filled with students, as usual, the majority white. Rabbit nudges CP, pointing out connected tables full of Hangout. The Hangout include their leader, Carlos, and his brother, Johnny Calabrese.
To CP

                    RABBIT
    You think Calabrese knows he was on tv?

CP examines the table of Hangout. Johnny quietly eats, while the others appear to enjoy Carlos describing his escapades at the Martin Luther King Jr. march.

                    CP
    You hungry?

                    RABBIT
    Naw. Not now.

CP instructs his followers to forget the food. They follow him to their chosen table where they draw close to receive further instructions. CP whispers directions. He then walks to the Hangout table.

                    CP
                  (TO JOHNNY)
    You gotta minute man? Can I talk to you?

Johnny looks up at CP and then to the rest of the Hangout group, who appear shocked but ready to defend themselves. Johnny points to the hall door. He takes a bite from his meatloaf.

He gets up. He walks with CP toward the lunchroom entrance.

          HANGOUT AT TABLE
Hey, Johnny! Whaat choo doin'!

          JOHNNY
Mind your own business.

          CARLOS
Aey, Pai-san! Don't forget your Italian roots over here!

          JOHNNY
You talking roots? The guy could be a cousin.

Takes a beat and then...

          CARLOS
Don't press your luck kid.

Johnny and CP continue out the lunchroom door.

INT. SCHOOL HALLWAY - DAY

          JOHNNY
What you want!

          CP
Got something important to talk about.

          JOHNNY
Yeah? What's dat!

          CP
Let me tell you something, man. I can see you're different. I got no problem about your girlfriend,

like some do. That's why I'm talking to you out here. But Martin Luther King Jr. is like family to all of us.

JOHNNY
Why are you telling me?

CP
I'm telling you because we can't let your brother and your family throw bricks at Martin Luther King Jr. and just forget about it!

Just then, there is commotion coming from the lunch room. A student exits. She runs from the lunchroom for help.

Shouts, punches, etc. are heard. Johnny moves toward the lunchroom. CP places his hand to block him. Johnny looks CP directly in the eyes.

JOHNNY
Move it!

CP continues to block his path.

CP
I figure you, and I don't have a beef with each other and don't need to be in there. You know how I like equality, and it's a fair fight.

JOHNNY
You don't want a problem with me, move your hand!

CP slowly steps out of Johnny's path. Johnny returns to the lunchroom as CP follows. There is chaos. Muscle-bound Carlos is holding one of CP's group over his head, while the others engage in battle.

There doesn't appear to be an obvious winner. It's a fair fight, until the school police officer and teachers run past CP and Johnny into the lunchroom, breaking up the rumble. Everyone is bloody including Carlos, with blood running from his nose. A couple of Hangouts help Carlos put on his leather jacket.

> CARLOS
> Hey, John, we still got your lunch over here, if you finished your talk with Martin Luther Coon over der.

The police officer and teachers separate the two groups. Johnny walks over to the table and removes a slice of bread from his plate. He stares at Carlos as he bites into it. Johnny then leaves the room alone.

INT. MS LITTLE'S HOME - DAY

Feminine hands pushing a thin brush through the cylinders of one of many pistols placed on a kitchen table. It's Linda with her two sidekicks. Miss Small, 240 pounds, forty-seven years of age, no lipstick, disheveled and sweating, exits a bedroom door, followed behind by a young muscle-bound Satan Lover "ROUGH RIDER." Rough is buckling his belt. He exits the two-story home.

> MS. SMALL
> What time Rabbit say they was gonna pick up these pistols?

> LINDA
> He already called while you was busy.
>
> They are running late.

Miss Small begins to place the pistols in a satchel.

MS. SMALL
Speaking of pistols, what was that boys name!

LINDA
They call him Rough Rider, Ms. Small.

MS. SMALL
You serious! That's *sho* who I thought he was!

DOORBELL RINGS.

SATAN QUEEN 1
I got it.

She opens the door. She returns to the table. Twelve young Satan Queens enter the room. Young girls aged thirteen through twenty enter the home, exclaiming, "Satan Queens! Satan Lovers!"

SATAN QUEEN 2
Miss Small, the Satan Queen! Lover Thang!

LINDA
Y'all sisters be cool. Have a seat. This gonna be short.

The Satan Queens quiet down.

Miss Small hands the satchel full of pistols to Linda and approaches mid-room.

MS. SMALL
Y'all sisters from Double 6 got some looking out to do. Sultan say those Viet Cong D's probably killed Mark, Kent, and William. He says they crib around 64th and Bishop. Right down the street somewhere.

Miss Small notices a young girl not paying attention, whispering to a home girl.

> MS. SMALL
> Child, you must be new up in here!
> Ain't no conversation when I'm talking. Who are you!

DAPHANIE, a real cutie-pie, aged sixteen, middle class, is just trying to hang. Daphanie wants to be accepted in the hood. All the happening girls are Satan Queens in her neighborhood. She has spirit.

> DAPHANIE
> My name's DAPHANIE.

> MS. SMALL
> Well, Ms. Daphanie, when the Satan Queen is talking, you best pay attention.

Linda has an eye for Daphanie.

> LINDA
> I got her in check, Ms. Small.

> MS. SMALL
> Somebody better have! Those Disciples killed my boy Ahmed, so sister Daphanie, when it comes to dealing with Ds, I take it real serious. Linda, you tell um what's up. I got to make a phone call.

Miss Small exits the room.

> LINDA
> Satan Queens!

LINDA SALUTES.

> **LINDA**
> This is what it is. Sultan wants all you cutie-pies to look out for new faces in the hood, especially coming in and out of 64th and Bishop. We gonna have a Set over here at Ms. Small's, and you gonna invite everybody we don't know.

There's a knock on the door, and Linda motions to Daphanie.

> **LINDA**
> Get it, baby.

Daphanie opens the door. It's CP and Rabbit with Alston Walker.

They all note the cute Satan Queen, cutest so far.

> **RABBIT/ALSTON**
> Man!

The three enter the home.

> **RABBIT**
> Where's Ms. Small?

> **LINDA**
> She's in the back calling you.

Rabbit and Alston proceed to the rear of the apartment.

CP to Linda.

> **CP**
> You tell um?

LINDA
I spoke about the Set. That's all.

CP faces the crowd of female gangsters.

CP
(Salutes)
Lover Thang! It's two of those Viet Cong D's out here, and they gotta go! So the only thang y'all fine-ass sistas got to do is hit on every dude you don't know in the hood and invite them to the Set.

Rabbit enters with a bag full of weapons and stands near CP.

CP
We know the Disciples are planning to come down on us big-time and real soon. That's what we're getting ready for. So anybody you even think might be a D over here, wire up Linda, and we'll handle it from there.

CP is looking at Daphanie.

CP
Later on. Stone Love! Lover Thang!

CP salutes. He, Alston, and Rabbit begin to exit the home.

Daphanie follows to lock the door.

DAPHANIE
Don't worry we're gonna hook y'all up, lover thang.

>   CP

Lover thang!

EXT. BIG BEAR LIQUOR STORE – DAY

The sidewalks are packed. Satan lovers move up and down the street in conversation.

INT. BIG BEAR LIQUOR STORE – DAY

CP, Rabbit, and Bobby China are talking with Mr. Mitchell, the store owner. CP cleans his dark glasses.

>   BOBBY CHINA
> You know we respect you and the store. That's why you ain't had no kind a problem in a long time. We're keeping those Disciples out of here, right?

>   MR. MITCHELL
>   (salt-and-pepper hair, blue-collar black man)
> Bobby, I ain't going into business with nobody!

>   BOBBY CHINA
> Look man, nobody trying to go into business with you! You been kicking down a Brick of Rose, crackers, and hog head cheese when you got ready, but now we need the cash, not the wine and lunch meat.

>   MR. MITCHELL
> Look, boy! I'm not paying any Disciples anything and no one else either. Never have and never will.

>   BOBBY CHINA
> If you don't pay Disciples, they kill you! You want us to act like that! And who you calling *boy*!

Bobby China opens his coat and displays his pistol.

CP Places sunglasses in his inside pocket.

> CP
> Calm down y'all. Richmond will be here in a minute, MR. MITCHELL. He'll straighten things out.

Daphanie enters, wearing her Satan Queen jacket, with tight-fitting pants. Bobby China covers his pistol with his jacket.

> BOBBY CHINA
> I don't care how long you've known me. You better watch your mouth.

Bobby China smiles at Daphanie.

> BOBBY CHINA
> Lover thang! Cutie-pie! Cutie-pie!

> DAPHANIE
> Can I talk to you, CP?

> CP
> Yeah, what's going on?

> DAPHANIE
> Can we talk outside?

> CP
> Come on.

They begin to exit when one-armed Lil Manny, waiting outside with Rough Rider, Andy, and several other Satan Lovers, opens the store door. Richmond and Sultan enter.

TO CP

> RICHMOND
> I need Double Six and everybody else on the Tray right now. We are leaving in twenty minutes. We wired up Rabbit.

CP signals a soldier with a Double Six Satan Lover jacket.

Richmond grabs Sultan's arm.

> RICHMOND
> I want the baby with me.

Sultan signals for one-armed Lil Manny and whispers to him.

Lil Manny takes off quickly.

> MR. MITCHELL
> Listen, Richmond—

A BIT AGITATED

> RICHMOND
> Later, man!

Richmond exits as Sultan follows behind. CP grabs Sultan's arm, getting his attention.

> CP
> Who's the baby!

Sultan smiles.

> SULTAN
> Aw. That's his semiautomatic sawed off 12-gauge.

Sultan exits.

TO DAPHANIE

                      CP
Catch me about 9:30 at the motel tonight. We can talk more.

CP exits.

INT. CAR – DAY

Rabbit is waiting behind the wheel of CP's Black 1965 Oldsmobile. CP and Bobby China enter the car. Bobby China rides shotgun.

TO RABBIT

                      CP
What's up! Where are we going!

                    RABBIT
Richmond owns a pool room over on 68th and Halsted and—

CP cuts in.

                      CP
68th and Halsted!

                    RABBIT
Yeah! Those Double Six Kings! They messing with his business. He's part-owner with his cousin.

Rabbit follows Richmond's caddy as it pulls away from the curb.

EXT. STREET – DAY

Five autos caravan eastward on 63rd street.

EXT. POOLROOM – DAY

The back of a sweater centered by a large crown atop the head of a coiled cobra, which is circled by the wording Double Six King Cobras. The sweaters owner opens the pool room door and enters.

INT. POOLROOM – DAY

It's a smoke-filled room, a multitude of jackets and sweaters with the Double Six King logo throughout, whose owners play pool or involve themselves in conversation. In the front of the room near the cash register, a Double Six King chief wearing an expensive Italian knit is waiting for change.

> DOUBLE SIX KING CHIEF
> Old man, can't you count! I gave you a twenty-dollar bill! You owe me fifteen dollars.

The gang chief pushes past the elderly balding cashier. He reopens the cash register. He calmly removes all the cash. He hands half to an associate who laughs. The gang associate moves toward the exit. The gang chief pockets the rest.

> DOUBLE SIX KING COBRA ASSOCIATE
> Thanks, man.

EXT. STREET – DAY

The Double Six King Cobra associate walks out the door where he sees the caravan of Satan Lovers double parking. He ducks into a phonebooth across the street, as the SLs exit their vehicles. He hurriedly searches for change, inserts the coins, and dials. Before the group enters the pool room, they pass the one-armed Satan Lover called Lil Manny near the entrance. Lil Manny hands weapons to several Satan Lover's as they pass him.

INT. POOL ROOM – DAY

Richmond enters first, noting the Double Six King chief slapping the elderly cashier with the cash and continuing to harass the pool room employee. The Double Six King gang members initially do not notice Richmond followed by Sultan and CP. Richmond retrieves a pool stick from its holder near the room entrance. The Double Six Kings in the room begin to notice Richmond and the other two SL chieftains. Like a slow ocean wave headed toward shore, awareness of their presence travels throughout. Some begin to approach the three Satan Lovers, until they notice a sea of SLs begin to enter and encircle the room weapons in hand. The room becomes silent.

SULTAN
Don't move! Nobody!

The Double Six King Chieftain is surprisingly unimpressed with the SL entrance. He smugly watches Richmond approach him, pool stick in hand, silently pointing to the money in the leader's pocket. CP notices a DK sliding his hand under his jacket. CP grabs a pool ball from a nearby table and throws it, striking the Double Six King in the chest. He crumbles.

CP
(Calmly)
Now the next Poot Butt movin, gon git blown away.

TO BOBBY CHINA AND ALSTON

CP
Check they pockets.

Bobby China and Alston Walker remove cash from most. Pistols are removed from several DK gangsters and handed to attending Satan Lovers. Richmond snaps his fingers signaling Lil Manny to remove the Baby from under his coat and hand it to him.

INT. PHONE BOTH – DAY

The DK associate who exited the poolroom earlier is still in the phonebooth excited. He has dialed and hurriedly awaits someone to pick up. Finally.

> DOUBLE SIX KING COBRA ASSOCIATE
>
> Yeah, he's here, wid a bunch of 'em!

The DK appears to listen to instructions as he removes his 32-caliber pistol from his belt and checks to reconfirm it's loaded.

> DOUBLE SIX KING COBRA ASSOCIATE
> Uh uh, all right, I'll wait on 68th and Peoria.

EXT. STREET - DAY SAME

The Double Six King Associate replaces his weapon, hangs up the phone, and confirms he's not being watched. He proceeds quickly down the street and around the corner.

INT. POOLROOM - DAY SAME

Richmond places the pool stick on a table. He is now pointing the semi auto 12-gauge at the DK Chief with the money from the cash register.

CALMLY

                RICHMOND
Give me my money.

           DOUBLE SIX KING CHIEF
Man, I know who you are, but I ain't never seen you up here before. We know about those Viet Cong D's too, but they don't come around here either. Now. Two thangs! With all due respect! One, if we knew this was your place, we would've come to you about it. Two, Satan Lovers don't run a damn thang over here!

                RICHMOND
I didn't ask you for conversation.

I asked you for my money. Now if I have to ask for it again, um gonna take more than that, including all that heart you want to show you got.

           DOUBLE SIX KING CHIEF
I told you man—

Richmond suddenly fires six rapid rounds from the 12-gauge auto.

The noise is deafening but brief. He has pointed the weapon above the head of the DK Chief, who has fallen to the ground trembling in massive shock. He can barely move. Debris from the ceiling falls around him. This weapon is powerful and not common.

To Bobby China as he reloads.

                RICHMOND
Get my money.

Bobby China puts the collected weapons in his pants and is masochistic in his treatment of the downed Double Six King Chief. He slaps him and uses his ear to turn him around.

>BOBBY CHINA
>Snap out of it, man! Look at your punk ass. You done pissed on yourself.

Looking at Rabbit and Rough Rider, shaking his head.

>BOBBY CHINA
>Damn!

He roughly positions the Double Six King Chief where he will not soil his hands and removes the cash. Bobby China brings the cash to Richmond, who has completed reloading The Baby.

>RICHMOND
>All right, let's go.

He motions for the elderly cashier to leave.

>RICHMOND
>Go home. I got another spot for you.

To the Double Six Kings.

>RICHMOND
>Y'all tell Chuck Akins, he owes me a month's receipts from outta here. He got three days to drop it off on 63rd. Now check this out. Y'all ain't got no business even knowing nothing about Viet Cong D's unless y'all talking to 'em.

>DK MEMBER
>D Thang! Disciples!

> RABBIT
> Disciples! So what y'all saying?
>
> Y'all Ds now!

No answer.

The older man walks past the crew of SLs surrounding the room and leaves.

CP and Sultan exit the pool room after Richmond. They are followed by the remaining SLs watching their back.

As they exit, the DKs attend to their leader.

EXT. STREET OUTSIDE POOL ROOM - DAY

As the large entourage turn a corner and approached their double-parked cars, they are met by seven more Double Six Kings standing in front of them. The Kings have their hands inside their coats and jackets appearing ready to draw weapons.

> CHUCK AKINS
> What's up, Richmond! What the hell you doing this side of Racine! Oh! You thought you could come through and put some fear in my heart! D Thang punk!

> RABBIT
> That's Chuck Akins!

At this moment, all seven DKs pull weapons. Simultaneously, approximately twenty Devils Disciples wearing Disciple jackets come behind the DKs, exiting from the gangways between the apartment buildings. Upper windows open from two adjoining buildings. Firearms are pointed from them. Richmond removes the Baby from under his coat. He cocks it and signals to the nearly twenty Satan Lovers behind him.

RICHMOND
Take 'em out! Get to the rides!

He fires toward Chuck and the enemy in front of him. Sultan and CP flank Richmond, pistols drawn and firing. The DKs and Ds spread out. Their weapons return fire. Chuck somehow escapes injury and fires his pistol wildly as he runs for cover.

CP
Get Richmond to his car!

Sultan taps Richmond on his shoulder and signals to follow him. Bullets wiz by from a brazened Disciple refusing to take cover. Sultan takes aim and subjects multiple strikes to the gangster's upper legs, knocking him backward. The Disciple loses hold of his 32 revolver. CP realizes his entertainment career is dimming.

CP signals for Rabbit.

CP
Rabbit! Help us cover Richmond!

The sea of SLs move toward their cars. Most are firing in the direction of the scattered Ds and DKs.

Richmond and Sultan make it to Richmond's ride. The rear door is already open in wait. Sultan holsters his twin guns. Richmond hands him the Baby and gets in. Richmond's driver already has the car in motion as Sultan slams the door, firing the Baby toward the enemy as he runs alongside his chief's auto.

Sultan approaches and ducks behind his auto, which was parked near Richmond's car, and removes 12-gauge shells from the ammo belt attached. CP and Rabbit have reached their car parked behind Sultan.

CP

Richmond missed Chuck Akins. Ain't that a trip. Double Six Kings turned Disciple!

SULTAN

They're Disciples, and we're Stones now. No question.

Sultan notices a rifle muzzle stemming from a second-floor apartment. He fires the full load, seven rounds from the semi auto in a fraction of a second. The sound is deafening but brief. A body crashes through the window and falls to the ground from the upper level. Sultan points at the fallen enemy.

SULTAN

Damn, that was just like in the movies, uh!

CP

Catch up with Richmond, and make sure he's okay. I'll get us out of here.

SULTAN

Stone Love!

He tosses the Baby in the car hops in. He ducks. He takes off.

CP reloads and is signaling for the SLs to leave. The SLs haphazardly pull away. The rear window of CP's ride is blown out with a shotgun blast. Rabbit has been in the driver's seat, ducking bullets and beckons CP to get in the car. He's a little nervous.

RABBIT

C'mon, man!

The Ds and DKs continue to fire from positions behind autos and the gangways of apartment buildings.

CP returns fire from behind his open car door.

> CP
> Satan Lovers! Satan Lovers!

SL Autos pull off, leaving a remaining three cars including CP and Rabbit. Rough Rider and Andy are pinned down behind a small brick wall on the porch of a two-story home, not far from their waiting auto and companions. Two DKs fire toward the porch from the side of a building across the street. Andy and Rough are lying low on the porch behind the brick banister, reloading a 45 auto and 32 revolver. Bullets ricochet from the brick wall protecting them.

> ANDY
> The only ones who know we're here are those two punks across the street. Ain't nobody popping at us but them!

> ROUGH RIDER
> What we going to do!

> ANDY
> We going to get to the car before they leave us. You loaded?

Rough Rider puts in the last 32 shell. He's fully loaded.

> ROUGH RIDER
> Yeah.

> ANDY
> When I say go, we gon run to the car and make them keep their heads down.

Keep shooting at 'em and don't stop!

Ready!

Rough Rider nods. Andy signals to their car.

> ANDY
> Go!

Andy and Rough Rider blast at the DKs and Ds as they hop from the porch and run to their vehicle. The enemy teens do as expected and duck to avoid being shot.

As the duo run to the car, they do not see the young Disciple gangster wearing the distinctive black hat and white band. He is armed with a double-barreled sawed-off shotgun. He is positioned to the side of the building they are leaving. The Disciple youth had not fired a shot until now. He, without thinking, points the weapon at Andy running behind Rough Rider. The pellet blast hits Andy in his rear calf, and he falls. Rough Rider makes it to the car and joins the other two SLs Joey Hilcomb and Alston, returning fire from behind the car.

> ANDY
> That little punk!

Rough Rider comes next to the car, shielded.

To Joey and Alston

> ROUGH RIDER
> Get in, and back up!

They enter the car and begin to back up slowly toward Andy when CP and Rabbit pull alongside. CP moves outside using the car roof to fire at the enemy. Rabbit is using the auto as a shield for his brethren.

To Andy

>   CP
> Get in the car, and let's go!

>   RABBIT
> Yeah. Hurry up!

Sirens can be heard in the distance.

Andy is bloody and is limping but able to move with help. He's helped into the car as Rough Rider guards the area where the shot came from. He also gets in the car.

Rabbit ducking nearly to the car floorboards.

>   RABBIT
> Can we go now, man!

CP gets in the car.

>   CP
> I'm out of bullets anyway! Go!
> Go!

Sirens are much closer. Young Disciple gangsters run into the street firing at CP and Rabbit as they pull away.

>   CP
> Satan Lovers!

Rabbit's face is filled with relief and disbelief.

EXT. ALLEY - SAME DAY

In the alley behind the Big Bear, Sultan, CP, Rabbit, Rough Rider, and Andy have parked their autos under the El Track.

CP examines his damaged window, while Sultan questions Andy. They examine his wounded buttocks.

> SULTAN
> You sure you don't want to go to the hospital?

Andy trying to view the multiple pellets embedded in his upper calf. Rough Rider and Andy are actually pulling out some of the skin-deep pellets with their fingers.

> ANDY
> Naw, man. It's not bleeding that much.

> SULTAN
> All right. Get over to Ms. Small's. She knows to bandage you up.

CP and Rabbit ready Andy to leave.

To Sultan

> CP
> So we Stones now?

> SULTAN
> Yeah, Richmond joined Black P. Stone, and (Chief) made me a Main 21. We're taking on the name "Loverstone!" That's it, only Ds and Stones out here now. Even Vicelords out west and the Cobras in Robert Taylor Projects belong to the

nation. This is huge now, man. Thousands! Stone Love!

INT. BOBBY's MOTEL ROOM - NIGHT

Richmond, Sultan, and CP are present with drug dealer Ted. CP sits on a sofa, while Sultan slowly stalks the room. Richmond and Ted sit at a table. Ted is counting out stacks of money.

He's finished. Ted is dressed in typical "Superfly fashion."

> TED
> Take it.

Richmond does not look at Ted.

> RICHMOND
> All right, Ted. Now don't get wishy-washy on us!

Richmond looks at CP.

> RICHMOND
> We still got something for your ass, if you come flakey. Let him out.

Sultan provides what appears to be a designed three distinct knocks to the door. The door opens, and Big Joey Hilcomb is standing there.

Ted exits.

> RICHMOND
> He's trying to play both ends to the middle with us and the Disciples.
> Tell Big Man we gonna need him soon.

>   JOEY
>   CP, somebody been waiting to see you.

TO JOEY

>   CP
>   All right, I'll be there in a minute.

CP checks his pistol. Sultan turns on the TV. Richmond is placing the money in a bag and hands CP an envelope full of cash. We hear news announcer.

The program has already begun.

>   WEATHERMAN
>   So it's unusually warmer lately here in Chicago, especially in the neighborhood of Englewood. Here's Walter with more.

>   NEWSMAN
>   That's right, Tony. Chicago streets are heated as gunshots are heard on Chicago's South Side. Two members of the Double Six King Cobras street gang suffered gunshot wounds to their—

CP exits the room.

>   CP
>   Let me check this out. I'll be back.

INT. MOTEL RECEPTION AREA - NIGHT

CP exits the room. He walks to the motel reception area, which is flanked by two nineteen-year-old Satan Lover security personnel. He sees Daphanie sitting sensuously in a chair.

To CP looking seductively and amorously

                    DAPHANIE
    You told me to catch you here tonight. Remember,
    I needed to tell you something?

                    CP
    Come here.

EXT. STREET - NIGHT

Daphanie follows CP to his auto, which is missing a rear window from the earlier shotgun blast. CP opens the passenger door. She gets in. CP shuts her door. CP then cooly walks around to the driver's side and also enters the car.

INT. AUTO - NIGHT

CP starts the car. CP points to the damaged window.

                    CP
    Getting that fixed tomorrow. Let's take a ride.
    What you got to tell me?

CP pulls off in a dash. They travel through Ogden Park.

                    DAPHANIE
    I know who the Viet Cong Ds are.

                    CP
    Yeah! Where'd you get that information?

                    DAPHANIE
    In church.

CP briefly glances over at Daphanie. He doesn't respond. Daphanie's a bit uncomfortable to CP's lack of response.

> DAPHANIE
> I was at choir practice at Shiloh Baptist Church over on May street.

INT. SHILOH BAPTIST CHURCH - PREVOIUS NIGHT

Daphanie is walking up a flight of stairs toward the church balcony door.

> DAPHANIE (V.O.)
> The balcony is usually empty during rehearsal, but I was sitting up there the Sunday before and lost my glasses.
> I wanted to see if they were there when I heard—

Voices of sixteen- and seventeen-year-old Larry and Glenn Russell

> LARRY
> It's like the Green Beret or something. You know, spies or something. I'm just sayin. We should get like a tattoo—Viet Cong D.

> GLENN
> Man, I don't want to talk about that stuff now, and I ain't puttin no Viet Cong nothing on me.

> LARRY
> But that's what they calling us, man. You got that joint on you?

Daphanie enters.

DAPHANIE
S'cuse me. Y'all seen my glasses anywhere up here!

Larry looks at Glenn.

LARRY
How long you been there!

DAPHANIE
Why?! How long y'all been up here! Yall s'pose to be downstairs in rehearsal! Y'all seen my glasses!

Glenn looks under seats near him. He sees the glasses, reaches, and picks them up.

GLENN
Here they go.

He hands them to Daphanie. When she attempts to remove them from his hand, he holds on.

DAPHANIE
What!

GLENN
What's your name?

Larry shakes his head and exits.

INT. CP'S CAR - NIGHT

DAPHANIE
So bottom line, he's coming to Ms. Small's Set.

CP
And you heard him say they called 'em Viet Cong D's!

DAPHANIE
I couldn't believe it, but that's what I heard. He told me to meet him there at eight o'clock.

CP
All right, cool. Now forget you told me, and just meet him there at the set. Do you know where they live?

DAPHANIE
Yeah. They live with their mother somewhere on 64th and Bishop. I don't know the address.

CP
Yeah, I figured on Bishop somewhere.

DAPHANIE
They just moved over here. Their mother joined the church not long ago. Made them sing in the young adult choir.

CP
All right, I know how we're gonna handle this. Why you going through all this to tell me, instead of Linda!

DAPHANIE
Why do you think, CP?

Daphanie's sexy eyes are beckoning CP's to leave the road.

They do, and he makes a U-turn back to the motel.

EXT. MOTEL - SAME NIGHT

CP's ride is parked in front of the motel. Security SLs are still there.

INT. MOTEL ROOM - SAME NIGHT.

CP's 32-caliber pistol is near the bed. A montage of lovemaking is experienced by the gangster couple.

EXT. MS. SMALL'S FRONT PORCH - BASEMENT PARTY - SATURDAY NIGHT

Dozens of teens hang around on and near the porch in front of the Satan Queen's home. Miss Small stands on her front porch supervising her property. Music plays local Chicago hits, "Big Boy" by the Jackson 5, Curtis Mayfield, Jerry Butler's "Your Precious Love," Gene Chandler's "Duke of Earl," The Opals's "Does It Matter," etc. A red glow from the party light illuminates from the basement window. Daphanie is sitting on the porch stairs looking through the crowd and down the street. Suddenly Glenn approaches.

>   GLENN
> I'm glad you waited for me outside.
> We didn't say nothing about that.

>   DAPHANIE
> That's no problem.

Glenn takes a few beats examining Daphanie. He looks for any possible danger to him in the area. Glenn has no idea his Viet Cong D identity has been revealed. Daphanie examines Glenn. She can tell Glenn is a little uncomfortable.

>   GLENN
> I got a joint.

> DAPHANIE
> I don't smoke or nothing. Want to just go inside?

> GLENN
> Yeah, c'mon.

The couple enter the house party. They take rear stairs leading to the basement, the party center. 1960s R&B music continues. Glenn takes her hand, and they begin to slow dance. Daphanie feels something hard on Glenn's waist.

> DAPHANIE
> What's that!

> GLENN
> That's our protection from any dumb stuff.

Daphanie breaks off the dance and steps back.

> DAPHANIE
> That really makes me nervous, Glenn.

CP has been waiting, sitting in a chair placed in a corner of the poorly lit room. Daphanie signals that Glenn is armed by asking Glenn…

> DAPHANIE
> Is that a gun!

She pretends to pull a trigger. CP is watching.

GLENN'S A LITTLE EXCITED

> GLENN
> Shhh! Don't do that!

He pushes her hand down.

> GLENN
> Look. I don't know nobody here. Who you know?

Pointing to several girls

> DAPHANIE
> That's my cousin and her girlfriends over there, and I don't want no gun around them.

Suddenly, Satan Lover Shorty Roman and crew enter the room. Unknown to CP and Daphanie, Glenn recognizes Shorty Roman. The setup is spoiled. Glenn grabs Daphanie by the arm and attempts to get out of sight.

> GLENN
> Let's go!

RESISTING

> DAPHANIE
> Wait a minute!

> GLENN
> Just come on! I'll explain when we get outside. Let's go!

Glenn and Daphanie finally reach the door when Shorty Roman notices the couple moving out of rhythm with the other party participants. CP has been watching and suddenly appears next to Shorty Roman grabbing his shoulder.

> CP
> I know who he is. Somebody's looking for him when he comes out.
>
> Y'all stay out of the way.

CP leaves the group and steps toward the exit after Glenn and Daphanie.

EXT. MS. SMALL'S HOME - NIGHT

Glenn leads Daphanie away from the building.

> DAPHANIE
> Slow down! Where are you going!

> GLENN
> Let's go to my crib. I saw some trouble getting ready to jump off in there.

> DAPHANIE
> Trouble!

Suddenly from across the street were Bobby China (wearing wide-brimmed hat and suit jacket with Black P. Stone button) and several Satan Lovers in uniform (black jacket with Black P. Stone emblem, black pants with green stripe down the leg, and red beret called a SUN).

> BOBBY CHINA
> Hey Viet Cong!

Glenn sees the group. He pulls his weapon. Daphanie breaks away and runs toward Bobby China. Glenn runs opposite direction. Glenn fires his weapon blindly toward the direction of the approaching Satan Lover stones. Daphanie has turned her back to Glenn but points out Glenn to Bobby China, confirming who they are chasing. Suddenly, an unintentional bullet fired by Glenn strikes Daphanie in the head. She falls. Glenn continues running. Bobby China comes to her aid.

The others continue the chase. Shots are fired from both hunters and prey.

Bobby China attempts to hold Daphanie's head in his lap. CP reaches Bobby China. CP is in distress.

> CP
> Aw naw, man! Naw!

> BOBBY CHINA
> Damn! Ds can't shoot straight!

INT. BOBBY's MOTEL OFFICE - DAY

Sultan is meeting with five young men wearing Black P. Stone uniforms.

One of the five seated with Sultan, smoking a thin Clint Eastwood-type cigar, is tall, slim, with a pencil thin mustache. Wearing a black waiter jacket with BPS Logo, he has the chief status, wearing red stripes down his black pant legs. It is Bolt, Main 21 of the Black P. Stone Nation and chief of the 4 Corner Rangers, part of The Black P. Stone Nation.

TO BOLT

> SULTAN
> This is CP. CP, this is BOLT, Main 21, Four Corner Rangers.

CP hands Bolt a briefcase and salutes.

> CP
> Here you go, Chief.

Bolt and his crew salute. They exit.

                    SULTAN
I like those Suns. The red berets representing the rising sun. I want to start seeing all our people wearing them.

EXT. STREET - DAY

Bolt and crew exit the motel. They enter an auto pulling up to meet them. GIU police detectives Buchannon and Banks exit their unmarked police vehicle and approach the motel entrance. They walk up to the two Satan Lover stones guarding the entrance without hesitation.

                    OFFICER EDWARD BUCHANNON
Police! We don't want to kill anybody, so don't act a fool. Tell Sultan Officers Buchannon and Banks with GIU want to talk to him.

The SL guards quickly examine the officers and decide that they are cops.

                    SATAN LOVER 1
Hold on. I'll see if he's here.

                    OFFICER EDWARD BUCHANNON
Punk! I said go get him before I shoot you!

The SL guard believes him and quickly enters the motel.

INT. MOTEL - DAY

Sultan places cash into a satchel, while CP and Bobby China count the cash contents of a separate briefcase, when there is a knock at the door. Bobby China looks through the peephole. He opens the door.

> SATAN LOVER 1
>
> Two GIU detectives say they want to see Sultan, and they actin crazy!

> SULTAN
>
> They probably followed Bolt here. I got it. Y'all finish up.

TO SATAN LOVER 1

> SULTAN
>
> Tell 'em I'll be right there.

Satan lover 1 exits.

> CP
>
> Sound like the same two I told you about.

> SULTAN
>
> They just call themselves putting me in check. They're trying to get paid like everybody else. I'll be right back.

INT. POLICE CAR - DAY

Sultan is seated in the back seat of the unmarked car.

> SULTAN
>
> Like I told you before, Detective, anytime the GIU want to talk with me, I got no problem with it. Now that I'm a MAIN 21, I know things might be a little different between us.

> OFFICER EDWARD BUCHANNON
>
> I understand your situation is a little different here in Englewood. What do you call them,

Viet Cong Disciple Snipers? The little girl and your other boys who got killed don't leave you no other choice but to do what you got to do. I understand that. But at the same time, we got to do what we got to do, and that's to be a better gangster than you.

SULTAN

Detective Buchannon, yeah, we're Loverstone now, part of The Black P. Stone Nation. That's pretty much what you came over here to find out and now you know. But anytime you want to make things easy for everybody, let me know. Everybody wants to get paid. That's pretty much the bottom line.

OFFICER EDWARD BUCHANNON

Hold on, Mr. Loverstone, Mr. MAIN 21! If you ever pretend to even dream to ask me about being on your little dumpy payroll, I'm gonna have to show you who the real gangster is, and that's gonna be me! I'm gonna *take* whatever I need, and I'm gonna *kill* whomever needs killing.

SULTAN

I provide opportunities, Detective. I don't make threats. I appreciate you trying to keep the peace and all that, but if you're about finished, so am I.

OFFICER EDWARD BUCHANNON

I'm gonna be watching you and your friend CP. Be careful out there.
Now get out of my car.

As Sultan exits car

> SULTAN
> Thanks for keeping the neighborhoods safe detective.

EXT. ALLEY BEHIND PIZZERIA - DAY

Johnny returns to the Pizzeria. He uses his keys to enter the *rear* door alley entrance. He enters the public washroom. He closes his stall door. Demarco Portofini and Joseph Milano enter the washroom. Demarco begins to wash his hands, while Joseph lights a cigarette.

> JOSEPH MILANO
> So who's *you* now! Pontius Pilate, washing the sins from your hands?
> Ha! Ha! He was *Italian* too, right?

> DEMARCO
> Yeah, but Angelo's not exactly Jesus Christ. He's no more good for the family JOEY. He's gotta go!

John remains quiet in his closed stall. He's angry and inquisitive at what he hears.

> JOSEPH MILANO
> It's not that bad, this cocaine. You selling to doctors and lawyers, Amico Mio. This cocaine thing is gonna be big. We're all millionaires with this, no question. Just cause Emilio says no, my family's got to starve! He takes and takes. We need new blood. They're coming in from Jersey. Paid in full. They don't screw around. I'll be fishing in Florida Sunday night.

Demarco grabs a paper towel.

                    DEMARCO
    I know it's only business, but he is my cousin.

                 JOSEPH MILANO
    They're coming through the backdoor here.
    Double-check, DEMARCO! Make sure it's
    unlocked. It'll be quick.
    You're in Vegas, right!

Joseph opens the stall next to Johnny and dumps his cigarette.

                    DEMARCO
    Right.

Both Demarco and Joseph exit the washroom. Johnny can't believe what he's heard. He peeps to ensure they have left. Johnny exits out the rear. He returns to his car, sits a few seconds, and ponders. He hits the steering wheel with his palm, starts the car, and drives to the front of the Pizzeria. He enters. Carlos and his boys are at the pool table.

Carlos speaks to a Loafer as he watches John enter. Speaking as a connoisseur.

                    CARLOS
    Hey, Rick. Damn if It don't smell like a Moolie.

Looking at Johnny.

                    CARLOS
    I don't see one, but *damn* that smell.

Johnny continues to the table in the rear where his father, Joseph, Demarco, and other Mafioso are seated in heated discussion. Angelo with thick Italian accent.

EMILIO
Our thing in Las Vegas is okay, but the drugs are bad for business. We can make money without hurting families!

JOHNNY
Pops, I got to talk to you. It's important.

EMILIO
John, son. Look, I gotta some issues here. I can't talk to you now.

John grabs his old man's arm.

JOHNNY
But Pops—

Loudly.

EMILIO
John Boy! I can't talk now.

Angelo is embarrassed at his response. He looks at the men sitting with him and then back to Johnny.

EMILIO
John, give your old man a break. I gotta thisa thing now. I'll talk to you about your thing later. Okay!

JOHNNY
You're always looking out for me, Pops.

He looks at the group of men at the meeting.

> JOHNNY
> It's time I looked after you.

John exits. Emilio and others begin where they left off.

Joseph Milano and Demarco Portofini look curiously at Johnny and then to each other.

EXT. CEMETERY - DAY

Satan Queen memorial guards consisting of six Satan Queens dressed in all black with red "Suns" (berets) stand near the grave site. CP, Bobby China, and Rabbit (all black with red berets) are also present. Standing next to CP is Linda, dressed in a red, green, and black Dashiki with red beret, and Ms. Small (all black). Family and friends, including Barbara and Cynthia, are present. Last rites provided by Shiloh Church Minister Reverend Hamilton just ending.

> REVEREND HAMILTON
> And those who have excepted Jesus Christ in this life will see Daphanie again. There will be a repast at the church. The family thanks everyone for the cards and well wishes. I ask that you keep them in prayer.

As the crowd begins to dissipate, the Satan Queen memorial guards salute. (right closed fist pounds the left chest area)

> LINDA
> Satan Queens! Almighty Black P. Stone!

To CP

> LINDA
> That cutie-pie was a little square, but those punk Ds gonna pay for this!

Linda walks to the Memorial Guard. She signals her crew to follow her. Barbara leaves Cynthia and also follows Linda. Cynthia is stunned. Linda and Barbara converse.

CP is watching intently from a distance. Linda glances at CP as she hands Barbara a cigarette. She lights it. CP continues to watch a non-smoking Barbara become something else, a Satan Queen.

EXT. BOBBY's MOTEL, SATAN LOVER HEADQUARTERS - NIGHT

Cynthia, Johnny Calabrese, and Barbara park in front of the motel. Barbara now wears a red beret and black jacket.

EXT. AUTO - NIGHT

>   BARBARA
>   Wait here a minute.

Barbara gets out of the car. She walks up to Joey Hilcomb and the century posted in front. They salute each other. Cynthia and Johnny watch from the car as Barbara speaks to the gangsters. She then signals for her friends.

As Johnny passes Joey.

>   JOEY HILCOMB
>   Be careful, gray boy.

Johnny shakes it off.

INT. MOTEL ROOM - NIGHT

Rabbit and Bobby China are consumed in a card game. Johnny, the girls, and CP sit on a sofa just ending their discussion.

JOHNNY
I love my old man. That's the only reason I'm here.

Looking at Barbara

CP
Well, I know it's not because you love me.

BARBARA
We're asking you to help him if you can, Chief.

CYNTHIA
Yeah, we both are.

JOHNNY
Hey, man, like I said before, this is business. You help me, I'll pay you what I said.

CP
We don't need your business. I had a father too. I was too young to save him, but I respect you looking out for yours. Now you ladies can step out to the lobby while we talk. I think I have a plan.

The girls leave.

CP
They're coming through the alley rear entrance, right?

Johnny nods.

CP
This is what we're gonna do.

Suddenly Rabbit, still engrossed in the card game, slams the table with his winning cards. Rabbit and Bobby China have totally ignored the others in the room.

> RABBIT
> That's it! Another *fo hunert*!
> Boy, you need to go back to school!

EXT. CALABRESE PIZZERIA - NIGHT

Johnny's car is parked across the street. He watches Mafia crew chieftains exit their chauffeured vehicles and enter the pizzeria past Pauly Glaudini guarding the entrance.

INT. PIZZERIA - NIGHT

It is closed for regular business and the usual Hangouts members hanging around inside. Big wigs have come to Chicago for this important meeting. Joey Costello approaches a long table where Emilio Calabrese and company are seated. Angelo is just finishing a joke, in his thick Italian accent.

> EMILIO
> So, thisa Wisea guy gets to the police station and wants to speaka to the guy who breaksa in his housea the nighta before. So the deska cop says, "You'll geta your chance in court!"
>
> "No, no, no!" says the Wisea Guy. I wanta to know how he gota into the house withouta waking my wife! I've beena trying to do thata for years!

The group laughs as Joey Costello approaches.

                    EMILIO
Hey! You all know Joey Costello. He represents the Commission in thisa matter.

Emilio offers a seat and points to each gangster sitting with him.

                    EMILIO
This is Albert Casella, Jersey, Vini Marchitti, from our six friends in Detroit, Eugene Capotorto, Antonio Bucossi from New York, and my Consignor Benny Gervasi. We appreciate you and all a ya's takina time to come and iron out—what **I** think is a greata anda hugea misunderstanding.

Can I geta yous a drink dere?

EXT. ALLEY - NIGHT

In the alley behind the pizzeria, a dark auto with lights out coasts to a stop at the rear alley door.

Figures dressed in dark clothing exit the auto.

EXT. FRONT OF PIZZERIA - NIGHT

Johnny sits in his auto. His car is positioned as to see the side of the building where another auto blinks its lights once.

EXT. ALLEY - NIGHT

Vito Massarone and Little Stevie Rossini are parked in the alley behind the pizzeria. Vito and Little Stevie remove automatic weapons from the trunk of their auto. They quietly use a key to unlock the pizzeria rear door leading to the bathroom. They don't speak and use only hand signals. They slowly open the door. They briefly listen for a moment to anything coming from the bathroom. They slowly enter.

EXT. OUTSIDE CALABRESE PIZZERIA - NIGHT

Johnny exits his car wearing a long dark trench coat.

Johnny walks up to six-foot-five, 250-pound Pauly Glaudini guarding the front door.

> PAULY GLAUDINI
> Hey, Lil John, we got a meeting going on here. You know about it. What cha doin'? Yous guys can't be here right now.

Johnny speaks with respect.

> JOHNNY
> Pauly Glaudini. My old man really trusts you more than most. So I trust you too. So you gotta trust me!

John exposes the weapon from under his trench coat. It's Richmond's semi auto 12-gauge shotgun, the Babe. Pauly instinctively pulls his 45 from his shoulder holster. Johnny looks him in the eyes.

> JOHNNY
> Trust me! My pops is in danger. There's no time.

INT. PIZZERIA - NIGHT

Pauly locks the front door behind them. Johnny and Pauly walk toward the rear washroom of the restaurant.

INT. PIZZERIA WASHROOM - NIGHT SAME

The two Italian assassins walk silently toward the washroom door leading to the restaurant. They passed the first stall whose door suddenly flings open.

Outside Johnny has positioned himself and Pauly facing the rear washroom when they hear shots coming from behind the door.

IT SEEMS LIKE SLOW MOTION

The washroom door exiting to the pizzeria seating area suddenly opens. Little Stevie Rossini exits firing his weapon back toward the bathroom.

INT. PIZZERIA - NIGHT

The table of gangsters all pull their weapons. Benny pushes Angelo to the floor and guards him with weapon drawn.

>   JOHNNY
>   Hey, hitman!

Stevie points his weapon toward Johnny but is too slow.

"The Babe" fires three consecutive 12-gauge shots that sound like only one. Stevie is blown apart.

Vito comes crawling out of the bathroom, firing at the ghosts behind him. He screams in Italian.

>   VITO
>   Chi sei tu?!! (Translated: "Who the hell you are?")

A shot from the bathroom hits his shoulder. Vito screams in pain. Johnny points Pauly to the bathroom.

JOHNNY
They're my friends in there, Pauly. He's the last one. Get his gun.

Pauly kicks the carbine from Vito's hand and removes the 45 auto from his shoulder holster.

PAULY GLAUDINI
It's Vito Massarone out of Jersey!

BENNY GERVASI
You alright Emilio!

Emilio Calebrese is in somewhat of a shock but in control.

EMILIO
John! What the hell isa going on?!

JOHNNY
It was a hit Pops, ordered by your cousin Demarco and Joseph Milano. I tried to tell you!

ANTONIO and BENNY approach the bathroom, guns drawn.

ANTONIO
Who in the hell is in there!

Johnny blocks the bathroom door. He tosses in the shotgun to outstretched hands.

JOHNNY
My friends.

EMILIO
Demarco! John! What are youa talkin!

Johnny pointing to the wreathing body of Vito Massarone.

> **JOHNNY**
> Ask him.

Benny is examining Stevie and the damage from the shotgun blasting "Babe."

> **BENNY GERVASI**
> This looks like Little Stevie boss.
> Remember, I did work with him.

> **EMILIO**
> John. Youa sure about this!

Johnny points to the wounded Vito.

> **JOHNNY**
> Ask *him*, Pop. I gotta go.

> **EMILIO**
> Get outa here. I'll takea care of this.

> **JOHNNY**
> Right.

Johnny begins to exit.

> **EMILIO**
> Hey, son, Thanksa, kid.

Johnny smiles, beaming with pride, and exits through the bathroom.

To Benny

> EMILIO
> All right. Be a nice and aska thisa guy who sent him.

Benny kicks Vito in the face. Blood gushes everywhere.

> BENNY GERVASI
> You heard him!

EXT. BLACK P. STONE HEADQUARTERS. AKA THE CASTLE - NEXT DAY- NIGHT

INT. THE CASTLE, BLACK P. STONE HEADQUARTERS HALLWAY 63rd & Kimbark - NIGHT

CP, Bobby China, and Rough are standing in the hallway, waiting outside a private room where Sultan, Richmond, and the chief of Black P. Stone, are meeting. Black P. Stone security, with military helmets and Black P. Stone uniforms, also stand in the hallway outside the door.

The door opens. Sultan and Richmond exit.

RICHMOND TO CP

> RICHMOND
> The Calabrese Outfit rep says they owe you. They say as a favor to you, they hooked up Chief with seventy-five labor jobs working construction downtown. We getting fifteen of those, and the rest go to the Nation. Plus we get the cleaners on 63rd and Loomis. They hooked us up with a lawyer too. We kick them up a percent, and we

good to go. Go on in there. Chief wants to meet you.

The guards open the door, and CP enters.

To Richmond

> SULTAN
> CP making the right friends.

INT. FLORIDA RESTAURANT - NIGHT

Joseph Milano dressed in a Hawaiian shirt, eating spaghetti alone in a restaurant booth. A man and a woman pass his booth. The woman appears to accidentally drop her coat.

The man picks it up, but while he is bending out of view, he fires a pistol, silencer attached. He covers the pistol with the coat as he fires at Joseph when he passes. Joseph gets it directly between his eyes. In one motion, the couple has completed their task and exits the restaurant.

EXT. RESTAURANT - NIGHT SAME

A car pulls up for the assassin couple, and they make their getaway.

INT. HOTEL LOBBY - NIGHT

LAS VEGAS FLAMINGO HOTEL LOBBY. Demarco Portofini with two Asian chicks enters the hotel heading toward the elevator.

They laugh and joke, having a Las Vegas ball. They enter the elevator. They are the only passengers. The car stops two flights up, and the door opens. Carlos Calabrese is standing there. He holds the door open with his foot. He points a gun at his cousin. The Asian chicks freeze.

                    CARLOS
            Hey, cousin D! I'm making my bones. Guess
            whoooooz a Wise Guy today!

Demarco frantically, in total shock, reaches for his shoulder holster to no avail, one shot to the throat. The girls scream. One shot to the head. Carlos removes his foot, and the door closes.

INT. CAR - DAY

CP, Sultan, and Rough exits The Castle and enter into an auto. CP rides shotgun.

TO CP

                    SULTAN
            Got another surprise for you.

Sultan hands CP an envelope.

                    SULTAN
            Bolt says your Calabrese friends got a line with
            the police. They got a suspect on who killed little
            Daphanie, Kent, and Linda's brother.

CP opens the envelope.

                    CP
            Man! Home address, everything.
            All right, let's flush 'em out.

EXT. STREET - NIGHT

Shorty Roman, Rabbit, and Bobby China sitting in an auto outside the home where the two Disciple brothers Glenn and Larry reside.

Shorty Roman fires six quick blasts into the front door. Mrs. Russell screams. Larry Russell rushes into her bedroom to comfort her.

Shorty Roman drives away.

EXT. STREET - NIGHT SAME

Later that night on 6 Tray on a side street adjacent to the Big Bear Liquor Store, CP, Shorty Roman, Bobby China, Andy, and Rabbit are gathered with several other SLs in serious conversation.

Suddenly, about half a block away, shots are fired at the group.

LARRY RUSSELL AND GLENN RUSSELL

Disciples!

Glenn and his brother walk toward the group, firing their revolvers. They expect the group to scatter.

BOBBY CHINA
Okay y'all! Remember nobody run! Those Ds can't shoot straight.

The group begins to walk toward the gun-firing duo. Larry and Glenn continue to fire. Led by Bobby China, a portion of the SL group begins to run toward the gun-slinging brothers. An SL close to Bobby China is hit in his hand. He slows.

WOUNDED SL
Oooh, man! Get them punks!

Glenn and Larry are surprised at the SL Blitz. They begin to back up but continue to fire.

Larry's gun is empty. He attempts to retrieve shells from his pocket but realizes there is no time for such luxury.

> LARRY
> I'm out. Let's go!

He begins to run, as Glenn takes time to focus and aim. He is going to knock off at least one of these crazed SLs charging him, before he breaks. He's alone, and from behind, a shot is fired, hitting his skull. In the middle of the street, his body falls limp, and his spirit has moved on.

Standing over his body, with her 32 revolver in hand, is Satan Queen, Linda.

Bobby China and his brave crew reach the body. Bobby China kicks Glenn's empty shell onto its back.

> BOBBY CHINA
> Almost worked perfect. Only got one, though. I knew those punks couldn't shoot straight.

Sirens heard. They leave.

EXT. REAR OF TRIANON BAR CONTROLLED BY THE ROYAL DISCIPLES - DAY

Fifty or more Royal Disciples being addressed by Disciple spokesman Ludo. Royal Disciple CHIEF LARRY DAVEN and LARRY RUSSELL stand next to Ludo.

> LUDO
> The King says that we gotta take out those punk Satan Lovers across Racine. Those punks trying to turn everybody Stone over there. They shot up this Disciple's house.

Pointing to Larry Russell

                  LUDO
Tried to kill his Momma and killed his brother!!

The crowd responds.

                  LUDO
Ain't but two or three of them punks over there anyway! We got Supreme Gangsters, and Imperial Gangsters on the way from 69th Street. They joining *our* nation! Ain't no room for no Satan Lovers, Lover Stone, or whatever they are calling they self.

The Supreme Gangsters and Imperial Gangsters have arrived.

Seven autos pull up. Big Nose Reggie gets out of the lead car wearing a white jacket with a crown on his back encircled by the words *Imperial Gangsters*.

He is of medium build, having a short haircut and an unlikely conservative look, with of course a notable nose.

                  REGGIE
Gangster Disciples! GDs!

                  LUDO
Gangster Disciples, huh! Yeah, Reggie, I guess so. It don't flow saying it the other way. Y'all in the Disciple Nation now.

They hug and salute, crossing both arms, fist closed across their chest. Ludo points to the Supreme Gangster Chief still in his ride.

> LUDO
> Gangster Disciples!

Nearby, the Satan Queen herself, Mrs. Little, is entering a phone booth appearing to be an innocent mother with head scarf and laundry cart. She dials.

INT. BOBBY's MOTEL - SAME DAY

Phone rings in motel lobby. Joey Hilcomb answers the phone.

> JOEY HILCOMB
> Awright.

EXT. IN FRONT OF BOBBY's MOTEL - SAME DAY

CP and Sultan, with all immediate Loverstone family members, stand in front of the motel. Several autos are lined up ready for immediate departure. Joey Hilcomb opens the motel door. He waves to Sultan.

> JOEY HILCOMB
> They coming! Ds got seven carloads of Supreme Gangsters and a bunch of Imperial Gangsters with 'em.

> SULTAN
> Okay!

Sultan speaks to the group of SL Leaders

> SULTAN
> Awright! Everybody do what they're supposed to do, and we won't have a problem.

Sultan whispers to CP and walks to his car. CP gives those responsible leaders instructions.

                    CP
Okay, you all got 59th and Racine. We're gonna
hold down the Tray. Rest of y'all handle 67th
to 71st and Racine. They coming through with
those Imperial and Supreme Gangsters. All right?
Make sure your people are ready. We will let you
know if they all come down 63rd. If they do,
meet up on Loomis Street at the EL.

The members go to their cars. They show the Indy 500 how it's done. They speed off to their destinations.

Richmond exits the hotel. He tosses the Babe to CP.

TO CP

                    RICHMOND
We gotta do what we gotta do! Take care of the
Babe, CP. I'll be at The Bear.

Richmond reenters the motel. CP holds on to the Babe. CP then bows his head with a short prayer. Sultan watches CP. He smiles while shaking his head. CP raises his bowed head. He walks to his waiting auto.

Sultan's and CP's autos leave last. Rabbit is behind the wheel for CP. Shorty Roman is waiting for Sultan.

CP to Sultan.

                    CP
Let's go take care of the Tray.

They enter their perspective autos and take off.

EXT. REAR OF TRIANON BAR RUN BY THE ROYAL DISCIPLES - DAY

Larry Russell locks and loads his 45. Additional troops arrive.

>   LUDO
>   Let's go!

A flood of gangbangers fill the alleys headed toward an attempted extermination of the Satan Lovers.

Ludo uses hand signals pointing to the directions the groups are taking.

INT. CAR - DAY MINUTES LATER

While parked in front of the Big Bear liquor store, Shorty Roman is pouring himself and Sultan vodka and orange juice into plastic cups.

Sultan is in the back seat checking his 38 and infamous pearl handled 357s for readiness.

Suddenly, a young Satan Lover approximately thirteen years of age is out of breath as he runs up to Sultan's car window.

>   YOUNG SL
>   They comin' down the alleys. They only three
>   blocks down, passing Throop Street right now.

TO SHORTY ROMAN

>   SULTAN
>   Pour him a cup of orange juice.

Shorty Roman does as requested. He hands the cup to the out of breath youngster.

INT. CAR - DAY

Parked behind Sultan, CP sees the discussion in front of him.

He gets out to investigate. He walks to Sultan's car window.

> CP
> What's going on?

Sultan holds up his hand and signals to CP to wait a minute.

TO YOUNG SL SOLDIER

> SULTAN
> All right. Go on home, man. You did your part.

The boy leaves as instructed. Sultan continues with CP.

> SULTAN
> They just about here, but they are walking through the alleys. They're almost to Loomis Street.

> CP
> All right. Let's get people in the yards on each side of the alleys.

> SULTAN
> Remember, make it every other yard so we're not popping each other. Tell everybody to watch out for cross fire.

Sultan exits his car. CP and Sultan speak to their chiefs.

They watch the word spread as bodies move and autos return to the backyards on each side of 63rd Street.

Residents play their part by closing their windows, locking their doors, and pretending to see nothing.

EXT. THE ALLEYS UNDER THE ELEVATED TRAIN (EL) TRACKS WITH THE ADVANCING SUPREME GANGSTERS, IMPERIAL GANGSTERS, AND ROYAL DISCIPLES - DAY

Miller speaks to Ludo followed by their gangster constituents.

> MILLER
>
> Man, this don't make no sense. We damn near to Loomis and ain't seen nobody.

As the group crosses Loomis Street remaining in the alley under the El Tracks, Miller sees a figure standing in the middle of the alley about half a block away.

> MILLER
>
> You see that down there!

> LUDO
>
> He damn sure a Stone. You see his hat! I hope his ass stays right there.

Suddenly, they recognize the figure. It's Sultan standing defiantly in full Black Peace Stone regalia. He shouts.

> SULTAN
>
> That you down there Ludo!

Sultan laughs.

> LUDO
>
> Fire that punk up.

Larry and Miller take aim. Sultan salutes and yells.

SULTAN

Black Stone!

Suddenly all hell breaks loose. From each side of the alley, shots are fired from the yards. The Gangsters and Disciples are dodging shots from their left and their right. The GDs are confused and surprised but return fire. The GDs hide behind the El Track tiers, old cars, and anything that might stop a bullet. It's a free for all. Time appears to stop as everything appears in slow motion. GDs are running and shooting everywhere.

Linda with Barbara and two other Satan Queens under the Single Home backyard porches as trained, hand off weapons they have reloaded to their male counterparts. A ricochet slug hits Barbara. She bends over in pain. Linda comforts her. The GDs fight courageously. There are wounded on both sides.

CP is firing from behind an EL Train pillar, when he attempts to reload one of his pistols. He is suddenly charged by a Disciple firing his weapon, who believes CP is now defenseless. CP rushes to perform the quick draw taught him by Don Juan. He wounds and downs the oncoming Disciple, who receives cover fire from his companions. The wounded Disciple is pulled to safety.

There is a montage of the various individual battles throughout the alley battlefield. Ludo uses an El pillar to block flying led. A soldier near him is grazed in the leg. He signals for help to get the soldier and himself out of danger. He realizes that their surprise attack has failed. He waves for his members to retreat. The Disciples and Gangster's retreat, firing weapons as they move backward through the alley. Sultan completes a reload of his 357s behind another pillar. He fires at the retreating gangsters with his huge weapons. The shots are deafening.

Andy runs up next to Sultan, laughing as the enemy moves backward. He fires his 32 revolver. Andy bravely steps out from behind the El pillar, guarding Sultan and himself. He continues to fire his weapon. Suddenly there is a familiar young Disciple having received late notice of the retreat. He also has a familiar sawed-off, double-barrel shotgun. It's the same young Disciple from the earlier Double Six King firefight.

Andy sees the young imp.

> ANDY
> Damn!

Andy attempts to step back behind the pillar for safety, but too late. He's grazed again in the buttocks with several hot shotgun pellets.

> ANDY
> Owww! Damn, I don't believe dis!

Andy angrily directs his remaining ammo at the fleeing Disciple youth. He screams and fires the last four shells.

> ANDY
> Ah ah ah ah ah ah ah!

Sultan signals two SLs for help.

> FIRST SATAN LOVER
> Linda says tell CP Barbara got hit.

> SULTAN
> Okay. Get Andy back to Ms. Small's!

The messenger and a passing SL grab Andy's shoulder and assist him off the emptying battlefield and out of danger. Andy is still screaming.

                    ANDY
        That was the same stupid ass punk D who shot
        me befo'! No shootin' punk can't hit nothing but
        my ass!

Finally police sirens in the distance. The seven-minute battle, which seemed a lifetime, is over.

CP signals the SL retreat. Sultan reaches CP and whispers a message. CP's reaction is subtle, but he's concerned. A neighbor's third floor view from above discloses a scattering of bodies leaving the area, each side assisting their wounded. Police arrive. Linda assists Barbara into an arriving ambulance. Barbara is mobile. Just a flesh wound.

CAPTION: s/b SUPER: April 4th, 1968

INT. BOBBY's MOTEL BEDROOM - DAY

The telephone rings. CP is counting receipts. He answers the phone, which is placed on the table upon which he is working.

                    CP
        Stone Love!

CP listens and suddenly!

                    CP
        What!

He slams the phone down and turns on the TV. He watches news report. He checks multiple channels.

                WALTER CRONKITE
        (Actual Footage) Good evening. Dr. Martin
        Luther King, the apostle of nonviolence in the
        civil rights movement, has been shot to death in

Memphis, Tennessee. Police have issued an All-Points Bulletin for a well-dressed white man seen running from the scene. Officers also reportedly chased and fired on a radio-equipped car containing two white men.

Every channel reporter states that Dr. Martin Luther King is dead.

CP buttons up his BPS jacket, puts the money he is counting in an envelope, turns off the TV, and storms out of the room. Bobby China and Joey Hilcomb meet CP as he makes toward the front entrance.

> BOBBY CHINA
> I guess you heard already.

They open the door and see the street full of people. Some crying, some in a hurry, others walking in disbelief, and still others standing in heated group discussion. The air is full of sound from shouts to auto horns blending into a mixture of human and mechanical murmur.

INT. CALABRESE PIZZERIA - DAY

Carlos Calabrese, the new Don in training, now suited up, sitting with the same Mafia crew subject to his father. He's outgrown the Hangouts, who are now under his brother, Johnny Calabrese.

> CAESAR
> What do ya think about the Luther King thing? Got wacked. We got a problem?

> CARLOS
> Everything's still running like clockwork, only things is we take a break here on the South side and the West side. See what happens tonight and

tomorrow. We got the word their calling in the National Guard.

                    CAESAR
I hear they're burning down the West side and starting to go nuts the other side of Ashland.

                    CARLOS
We just let it play out. Where's Lil John?

                    CAESAR
Hey, John!

Johnny Calabrese is face down in a deep pan pizza surrounded by Hangouts. John uses a napkin, slides out the booth, and crosses to Carlos.

                    JOHNNY
Yeah!

                    CARLOS
You see the news?

                    JOHNNY
Yeah.

                    CARLOS
You know that other business! Your soul brother der. We got points due today? There's a lot going on. I'm just *askin*.

                    JOHNNY
He's a stand-up guy. You know that.

> CARLOS
> There's just a lot going on that's all I'm saying. We got points to kick up. You know, things gotta be right.

> JOHNNY
> Yeah, I know. I got pizza, Carlos!

> CARLOS
> I'm just *asking* John!

Johnny crosses back to his booth and pizza.

To himself

> CARLOS
> I love the kid, but the old man spoiled him, I swear. Pops retires back to the old country and leaves me to deal with this kid. He's out of control.

EXT. BOBBY's MOTEL - DAY

CP, Bobby China, and Joey Hilcomb stand in front of BOBBY's MOTEL.

CP's surveying the crowded street and apparent chaos.

> BOBBY CHINA
> Chief, we can't make that drop today in their hood. It's too crazy out here!

> JOEY HILCOMB
> Chief, those grey boys will understand. It's too hot everywhere.

Fire truck sirens. The burning and looting have begun.

To All Stones in earshot

>   CP
> Call came from the Castle. MAIN 21 passed the word. Can't be no rioting in areas we control. As far as those Grey Boys go, they take care of their business, we gonna take care of ours. Y'all stay here. Joey, check on my girl Barbara. See how she's doin'. Now get out here, and patrol our areas. No burning or looting anywhere around here.
>
>   JOEY
> Okay, Chief, but take my piece with you.

Joey attempts to hand CP his 32 revolver.

>   CP
> Give me your car keys, Joey, keep that pistol. Too hot now.

Joey reluctantly hands CP the keys and replaces his weapon in his belt.

CP smiles and walks toward Joey's black Thunderbird.

EXT. STREET - NIGHT

CP behind the wheel. He reaches 64th and Ashland Street, the border between black and white in the Southside Englewood Community. It's difficult to cross. Police cars and fire trucks screaming past between white on the West side of the street, black on the East. Rocks, bricks, and bottles are occasionally thrown one way or the other. The separated groups yell unintelligible insults at each other.

CP sees an opening and zooms across the street. Joey's car is barely missed by a couple of thrown missiles. CP turns toward the sound of breaking glass. CP does not notice the makeshift barrier in front of him. He grinds to a stop to avoid crashing into the wooden horses and garbage cans blocking the street. Before he can react, his driver's side door is snatched open, and multiple hands pull him from the car.

CP decks two of his attackers with a straight right hand and quick left hook. He is grabbed by a white fighter. A careless mistake by the fit and aggressive twenty-one-year-old Caucasian. CP smoothly uses the standing switch, slamming him face down.

As CP stands, he is tackled from behind by a courageous attacker and then held by all present.

Stan Manske, a tall, slim makeshift leader of the white street blockade, is almost nose to nose with CP.

>STAN
>What's your problem! You know you got no business over here. Martin Luther coon is dead. Don't you get the message!

>CP
>Your breath stinks, grey boy!

Stan pretends to turn his head and then suddenly punches CP in the gut. CP expected it and takes the punishment like a champ.

>CP
>Ugh!

The crowd is growing, and the white spectators shout with approval.

>STAN
>Should we hang 'em or cut his prick off?!

The crowd cries for both.

                           STAN
        Unzip his pants and give me a shiv.

As one guy unzips CP's trousers, another passes a knife. As Stan takes the knife, he slowly moves toward CP, reaching down toward his private area. Suddenly, three cars filled with Italian teens wearing leather jackets, jeans, and T-shirts pull up and park in the middle of the street. Johnny Calabrese wearing dark glasses slowly exits the lead vehicle.

CP thinks he has a reprieve but is not certain.

Johnny to Stan. Calmly.

                          JOHNNY
        Stan Manske, what are you doing Jack off?

Everyone there recognizes the Hangouts and Johnny Calabrese. Stan knows he is no longer in charge.

                           STAN
        Hey, John. We're gonna cut this coon's balls off!
        You want in!

                          JOHNNY
        Sure, gimme that!

Johnny holds his hand out for the knife. Stan immediately hands it to him. Johnny looks at CP. CP is not sure what to think. Time moves slowly.

                          JOHNNY
        Let 'em go.

Stan hunches his shoulders and gives the men restraining CP a look that says he has no idea what the hell is going on. They release CP with the encouragement of a couple Hangouts tough guys.

Stan almost laughs and cries in his confusion.

EXT. BOBBY's MOTEL - EARLY MORNING DAY

Detectives Buchannon, Banks, several other GIU detectives, and uniformed police bursting through the motel entrance.

>GIU/POLICE
>Police! Don't move! Chicago Police Department! Don't move!

INT. BOBBY's MOTEL ROOM - EARLY DAY

Officer Buchannon and uniformed police burst into a motel room where CP is sleeping.

>OFFICER EDWARD BUCHANNON
>Police! Off the bed and on the floor, CP! You're under arrest!

EXT. BOBBY's MOTEL - EARLY DAY

In front of BOBBY's Motel, CP, Joey Hilcomb, a limping Andy, Bobby China, Rabbit, and Shorty Roman are handcuffed. They stand backs turned to the detectives who read them their rights.

>CP
>Buchannon! I want to call our attorney before we leave. Just want to save time posting bail.

> OFFICER EDWARD BUCHANNON
> Bail! You don't get a bail bond for first-degree murder, son.

The group of thugs turn their heads simultaneously.

> JOEY HILCOMB
> Murder! You got something mixed up officer!

> OFFICER EDWARD BUCHANNON
> You are all under arrest for the murder of Glenn Russell. You can make your calls from the station. Sultan's got an alibi, so call *him*. He can call your families.

A paddy wagon pulls up, and the SLs led inside it.

INT. COOK COUNTY JAIL - DAY CAPTION: S/B SUPER: SIX MONTHS LATER

CP in a cell, shivering under his blanket, as he lays upon his cell bunk. Andy is his Cellie, shouting through the bars down the Catwalk.

> ANDY
> My Cellie's sick! He's got a fever! He been hot as fire for two days now. Y'all gon do something!

A Screw finally shows up. He looks at CP through the bars. He can tell it's no joke. Speaking on his walkie-talkie.

> SCREW/GUARD
> Need inmate transport to the hospital.

INT. JAIL HOSPITAL - DAY

Thirty-three hours later: CP sits up in his bed. He's eating lunch and doing much better.

Another inmate is in a bed next to him, thirty-three-year-old Black Panther Bobby Seale.

>BOBBY SEALE
>
>You all right, brother? They said you had pneumonia.

>CP
>
>Yeah, man, I'm all right.

CP recognizes the inmate next to him from TV News.

>CP
>
>Man! You that Black Panther, brother. I saw you on TV back on the tier.

>BOBBY SEALE
>
>Yeah, that's me, brother. Out here to see brother Fred Hampton. They're holding me for a minute. I got a little health problem they're checking on. I'll be out in a day or so. How long you been in here?

>CP
>
>Two days in the hospital. Almost six months now on the tier.

>BOBBY SEALE
>
>What do you know about the Black Panthers, my brother?

                    CP

Yeah, y'all trying to make carrying guns legal or something.

                BOBBY SEALE

That's already legal, my brother. But that's not the only thing we're about. We're not about using guns against each other, my brother. I heard one of the guards say you were a Black P. Stone, right?

CP takes the last bite of his lunch.

                    CP

Right. Representing Loverstone.

                BOBBY SEALE

Chairman Fred Hampton is trying to work in Chicago with your organization now. You're representing the wrong thing if you're killing your own, my brother. You don't see Italian gangsters doing as much damage as we do to our own people. That's because they understand family, because they understand their language, culture, and history. We were the only slaves to ever have all that removed as a people. We've got to get away from a slave mentality.

They are interrupted by a Screw entering the room.

                SCREW/GUARD

Let's go, Stone. You're going back to your tier on E4.

CP gets up and prepares to leave.

> BOBBY SEALE
> Think about what I said, brother. My name is Bobby Seale.

> CP
> Yeah, man. I'm CP. I'll think about it.

INT. COOK COUNTY JAIL - DAY

Barbara, Cynthia, and Johnny Calabrese enter the jail visiting area. CP enters the reverse side of the steel booth separated by a thick hard plastic window. Holes in the steel plating under the window are used for talking.

> BARBARA
> My grandmother doesn't know I'm here. I couldn't come before now—

> CP
> That's all right. How you been doing?

> BARBARA
> I'm fine. You get my letters?

> CP
> Yeah, everyone. Hey, John.

(John nods in response)

> CYNTHIA
> John has some good news. Tell him, baby.

> JOHNNY
> My old man made some calls when he heard. They don't have nothing on none of you. Up to

now, you've been refused bond because they just want all Blackstones off the street.

BARBARA
I heard it was all connected. There's like this big thing against the Black Panthers, student protest groups, Black P. Stone Nation, and anti-Vietnam War groups.

JOHNNY
Yeah, on TV news, they're calling it a national security problem. Anyway, my old man's lawyer says you'll get a bond on your next court date.

CP
They got us Satan Lovers spread out on E block. Blackstone tiers. The jails full of those protest people too. We had Dick Gregory on the tier for a minute. I see the news talking about the riots and all that stuff. Yeah, this Stone tier stays full.

JOHNNY
Just wanted to let you know that. We'll wait outside and let you two talk.

Johnny takes Cynthia by the hand. They signal a curious Screw and exit.

Barbara and CP look at each other for several beats, one expecting the other to speak first.

BARBARA (to CP)
I really miss you...

I'm really glad to see you...

I'm sorry...

(They really don't know how to start, but after a few beats.)

> BARBARA
> What are you going to do with your life?

> CP
> Yeah, I think about it a lot. I see the same brothers come in on the New every other week.

INT. COOK COUNTY JAIL - DAY

Scene fades to earlier on the tier. CP and other inmates sit on one of the picnic tables in front of the television. Tier gate opens. Three young men enter.

The inmate sitting next to CP announces.

> INMATE 1
> On the New!

One of the three inmates enters the tier.

> WILLIE
> On the new again y'all! Stone Love!

> INMATE 1
> Willie back y'all!

Willie walks toward CP and the other inmates at the table.

> WILLIE
> CP! What's up! Stone Love, man.

They salute and hug.

> CP
>
> You been back here three times since I been here. I forgot what your first beef was.

> WILLIE
>
> It was a murder beef. They dropped the charges, no witnesses. Y'all had pork chops yesterday, right?

> CP
>
> You been back here about once every two months! Man, all they got to do is let me out of here once. What kind of beef you got now?

Willie gets comfortable, as if he's never left the tier.

> WILLIE
>
> Same thing. Tempt murder. Food come up yet?

CP leans back and looks at his institutionalized inmate associate in amazement.

> CP
>
> Naw, man, you just in time.

INT. COOK COUNTY JAIL -DAY

The scene fades back to Barbara and CP in the visiting cage.

> CP
>
> It figures, ya know? If you get out and keep doing the same thing, going to the same places, you gonna have the same thing happen.

> BARBARA
>
> So when you get out, what are you going to do?

CP

They let us put together shows in the chapel, singing and stuff once a week. I'm gonna try and keep singing, but right now I just want to get out.

Lt. DANNY ROBINSON enters CP's side of the cage

LT ROBINSON
(Correctional officer)
Visiting is over. Wrap it up, CP.

CP

All right, lieutenant!

Barbara and CP touch the vent under the window. CP turns to leave.

LT. ROBINSON

You been practicing that straight hand I taught you?

CP motions for Lt. ROBINSON to raise his hand. CP throws two quick jabs and a hard straight right-hand punch to the palms of Lt. ROBINSON's hands. Repeats the action.

CP

How long you been cornering for Muhammad Ali?

LT. ROBINSON

A little while. Since he's been in Chicago. Now if you want to stay outta jail, when you get out, I'll work with ya.

                    CP
Yeah, I'll think about that, lieutenant. If throwing hands will keep me out of jail, I might do that.

EXT. STREET - DAY

Five Disciples, including Larry Russell, Miller, and Kilman dressed Gouster style, exit a building carrying illegal cargo.

Both marked and unmarked police cars swoop in. They surround the group. Larry and his crew are handcuffed. The group are placed in a paddy wagon.

INT. SHILOH BAPTIST CHURCH - DAY

We see Rev. Hamilton servicing his congregation. His lesson is nearing its end.

Barbara and Cynthia sit together in a pew behind Mrs. P.

              REVEREND HAMILTON
So allow me to end by saying, without commitment, you have nothing. If you are unable to commit to anything, who can depend on you? But we are so blessed that God committed the life of His only begotten Son so that we have the opportunity to live.

Let's accept this opportunity and accept everlasting life. Let's surrender ourselves to God, through His Son, Jesus Christ, and pray for those gang members caught up in death and destruction. God bless you.

MRS. P

Amen.

The congregation begins to dissipate as Barbara and Cynthia walk to Mrs. P.

BARBARA

Hi, Mrs. Powers.

MRS. P

Hi, child. How are you? My prayers were with you after what happened.

BARBARA

I'm doing well. This is my friend Cynthia.

CYNTHIA

Hello.

Mrs. P nods.

MRS. P

Did you all enjoy Rev. Hamilton's message?

BARBARA

Yes, mam. I wanted to tell you I went to visit CP.

MRS. P

That's good. I know he's gonna be alright.

BARBARA

Yes. He's doing fine.

MRS. P

He should be Barbara. I've been praying for the safety of all my sons every day since they came into this world. I'll be in court. I've placed his care in God's hands, and that's all I can do.

BARBARA
I think he really wants to change his direction in life.

MRS. P
I continue to pray for him every morning and night. The Lord's going to take care of him. You can depend on that.

BARBARA
I'll keep praying too, Mrs. Powers.

Mrs. P gathers her Bible. She excuses herself. As she exits, she drops her church program. Larry, Russell's mother, picks it up and hands it to her.

MRS. RUSSELL
Here you are, sister.

Mrs. P nods a thank you and then returns her gaze to Barbara and Cynthia.

MRS. P
God bless you both.

INT. APARTMENT BUILDING HALLWAY - NIGHT

Larry Daven and three Ds standing masked outside a drug dealer's door.

Their female flunky, Flora, knocks on the door for a drug sale.

> FLORA
> It's Flora. I need one.

When the door is cracked open, Larry kicks it in, leading several masked and armed Disciples to invade the residence. Flora exits the scene.

Larry shoots and wounds to the leg the drug dealer who attempted to reach for his weapon. The remaining Ds, dressed in all black, speedily ransack the apartment for cash and drugs.

The wounded drug dealer lays bleeding and attempts to communicate with the intruders.

> WOUNDED DRUG DEALER
> C'mon, man, I recognize y'all. I know you all Disciples. You're Larry Daven. You already been paid.

Larry Daven and his companions look at each other. Larry returns his gaze toward the wounded drug dealer. He lowers his mask, revealing his face, shakes his head, points his weapon, and fires to the face.

> LARRY DAVEN
> Damn

INT. COOK COUNTY JAIL BULL PEN - DAY

CP wears suit, shirt, and tie. He is standing with both hands grasping the bars as he gazes outside a window awaiting freedom. Suddenly, a Screw opens the bullpen gate and Royal Disciple Chief Larry Daven, Miller, Kilroy, and three Disciple soldiers walk in. CP notices their entrance and then continues his gaze outside their world.

Royal Disciple Chief Larry Daven can't believe he's looking at CP, his schoolmate from fifth grade. He whispers to the large six-foot-three Disciple in his group who approaches CP.

>   DISCIPLE INMATE 1
> You CP!

CP turns and faces the D. He moves away from the bars. Somehow he knows God is on his side. He displays no fear.

>   CP
> Yeah.

>   DISCIPLE INMATE 1
> You kill Glenn Russell!

>   CP
> That's my beef.

CP turns and faces his challenger.

>   DISCIPLE INMATE 1
> Why you backing off the bars! You want to humbug or something!

CP knows there is more detriment with a no answer.

>   CP
> Yeah!

The Disciples minus Larry slowly approach CP, but Larry signals them to stop. He is the highest rank of the group inside the bull pen.

>   LARRY DAVEN
> Hold on! We no punks! It don't take all us!

Disciple Inmate 1 and CP throw up their dukes. CP wastes no time to utilize the small skill learned from Lt. Robinson.

He throws a hard straight left-hand jab, followed by an unstoppable right. They both hit their mark to the face of his opponent. The tall Disciple was bluffing. He has depended on his size to intimidate. He has no heart and can't box. He knows nothing else but to grab CP and attempt to wrestle him down, which is very unfortunate for Disciple Inmate 1. (Remember CP has competed as a wrestler since age eleven and remembers the standing switch.) CP performs the standing switch beautifully. His opponent hits the ground with both his weight and CP's, face-first. He's almost unconscious as CP punches and kicks his face in.

The Disciple's rappies come to his rescue and pull CP away.

Their six-foot-three rappie's face is bloody, and two teeth are missing.

LARRY DAVEN
Let him go!

Larry points to a five-foot-eight Disciple, with processed hair, in the group. He has obvious boxing skills as he holds his hands like a pro. He's short but fast. A punch to CP's jaw and liver. CP goes for what he knows. He grabs the long-processed hair to steady this opponent's head and then punches hard and steady. They fall to the ground. The Disciple has no chance. Again the Disciples who remain come to their partner's rescue.

Just then, a bailiff enters, and the Disciples back away.

BAILIFF
Charles Powers. Let's go!

CP, with a torn, bloody shirt and all, follows the bailiff's instructions, as he tries to tidy up as best he can, to appear before the judge.

INT. COURTROOM - DAY

CP enters the courtroom escorted by a bailiff.

                    MRS. P
          My son!

Gasps are heard in the courtroom.

CP stands with his attorney in front of the judge, a bit embarrassed by his mother's outburst.

                    JUDGE
          Are you all right, son!

                    CP
          Yeah, it's not my blood.

INT. COOK COUNTY JAIL HALLWAY - DAY

CP is being escorted back to his tier, handcuffed, by a Screw.

He stops CP in a secluded area.

                    SCREW/GUARD
          So you the punk Stone that think you so bad!

The screw punches CP on the side of his face. CP is wise enough to simply cover up. If he wins the fight and injures the screw, he can look forward to ongoing beatings and harassment from other screws and just another beef to fight in court.

EXT. MRS. P'S HOME - DAY

Barbara rings Ms. P's doorbell. There are two SLs standing outside guarding the home. The door opens. Both Randolph and Eddie exit carrying suitcases heading to a car parked in front.

Randolph looks PO'd. Eddie is the only one with manners.

> EDDIE
> Hi!

Eddie continues to struggle with his suitcase to the car, and Mrs. P comes to the door with a smaller bag.

> MRS. P
> Hi, baby! You all right?

> BARBARA
> I thought I'd stop by and see what happened in court. Did they set CP's bond?

> MRS. P
> Well, as far as that, things look good. I believe in the grace of God. His lawyer says that the prosecutors can't really produce any witnesses, so the court had to set a bond for all of them. CP's friends are going to pay the five thousand dollars, so I'm not worried about CP right now. I've got to make sure the two children left in my home are safe.

The Satan Lover security reach out. They offer to carry the bags in Mrs. P's hands. She gladly hands them over.

> BARBARA
> What do you mean, Mrs. Powers?

> MRS. P
> Well, Randolph and CP look so much alike, they've been shooting at him, thinking he's Charles. I'm sending them both to Piney Woods boarding school in Mississippi.

Mrs. P locks the door behind her.

> MRS. P
> I'm taking them to the train station right now. You be careful okay, honey!

Mrs. P doesn't wait for an answer. She hurriedly walks to the car, enters, starts the motor, and pulls off. Barbara waves.

INT. COOK COUNTY JAIL TIER - NIGHT

On the Blackstone Tier E-4, CP and other inmates are eating dinner on the picnic benches inside the tier. The infamous Babystone approaches. A sixteen-year-old charged with double murder and the highest ranked by their BPS Chief on the tier sits next to CP.

> CP
> What's happening, Babystone?

> BABY STONE
> Two Mains sent word. They want you to come down to Chapel tonight.

> CP
> Main 21s, who?

> BABY STONE
> Big BOLT and your chief, Sultan.

I already told the Screws to put you on the list.

                        CP

All right.

INT. COOK COUNTY JAIL CHAPEL - NIGHT

CP and several inmates enter the jail Chapel. In the last rear pew are Main 21's, BOLT, and Sultan. Both wearing formal BPS uniforms with two Black P Stone emblems. They are wearing black pants with a red stripe. BOLT, in his early thirties, is again holding an unlit Clint Eastwood type cigarillo propped in the corner of his mouth. Bolt signals CP as he enters.

To Sultan

                        BOLT

There's your boy.

CP sits next to Sultan.

                        CP

What's happening, Chief?

                        SULTAN

When I get out, I'm gonna have to leave the city for a while. You're gonna be running things while I'm gone. Richmond is behind you. The Family knows.

                        BOLT (To CP)

I heard about you representing in the bullpen. I like you, young blood, you all right.

                        SULTAN

I know you gonna take care of business for me.

(Sultan salutes)

                    SULTAN
          Stone Love!

CP returns the salute. CP faces forward. He looks into himself.

EXT. COOK COUNTY JAIL - DAY

CP exits the jail. Barbara, Cynthia, and John are waiting.

Behind them in Sultan's personal ride is Satan lover 1, sitting behind the wheel wearing his red beret and complete Black P Stone uniform. Don Juan, who is also in full BPS uniform, holds the open rear passenger side door. CP and Barbara embrace. CP shakes John's hand.

Staring at the waiting auto.

                    BARBARA
          Ride with us. I've got dinner and some special
          things waiting for you!
          I'm out of that mess now. You can get out too.
          Come on.

CP looks deeply at Barbara.

                    CP
          I wish I could, but I can't right now.

Barbara pleads. Barbara begs. Barbara cries.

                    BARBARA
          Don't go with them. You said you wanted to go
          in another direction when you got out. Be that
          singer, and be that actor in Hollywood.

> **CP**
> And I still plan to do that. I just need a little time to put some money away and travel to—

Barbara interrupts.

> **BARBARA**
> John's father says he can fix you up with a regular job. You can go back to school and get away from that. My heart is for you, CP. I think you know that. Come with us.

Pointing at the waiting auto, Barbara again stares at the waiting car and back to CP's serious gaze.

> **BARBARA**
> Come with us please.

CP kisses her forehead and begins to walk toward Sultan's car. Barbara looks on with anger, humiliation, and disgust.

> **CP**
> I'll get with you as soon as possible.

As he approaches the car, GIU detectives Buchannon and Banks drive their unmarked police car between CP and Sultan's car.

> **OFFICER EDWARD BUCHANNON**
> Leave with your girlfriend and start a new life somewhere else, CP. You got the federal government involved out here now. A lot has changed, and Black P. Stone is going down. You can be certain of that. We talked to Danny Robinson. You got some people out here in the boxing world who like you and want to help.

You should take advantage of that.

CP
I don't mean any disrespect detective, but you want to watch out for my toes? You damn near ran 'em over.

OFFICER EDWARD BUCHANNON
You're not a bad kid, CP. Think about it. We'll be watching you.

Buchannon and Banks drive off. CP enters Sultan's auto as Don Juan holds the backdoor open. Barbara breaks down in tears.

Don Juan salutes and closes the door after CP enters.

Don Juan hurries around to ride shotgun. They pull off with CP now in full control of the Satan Lovers, aka Lover Stone, a faction of the Black P. Stone Nation.

Montage of CP taking on the duties of the Satan Lovers leader.

EXT. GARAGE - DAY

A trailer truck and three stolen cars are directed into a mafia-controlled garage. Shorty Roman is in the lead vehicle. The doors close.

INT. MOTEL ROOM - DAY

Surrounded by Andy, Joey Hilcomb, and Alston Walker, several obvious pimps and drug dealers stand in line, submit their street taxes, and shake CP's hand while handing him their money-filled envelope.

INT. CALABRESE PIZZERIA - DAY

CP enters and hands Carlos a cash-filled envelope. Carlos is sitting in a booth. Carlos hands CP a typed document. Just a business demeanor only.

> CARLOS
> Here's the Balboa jobs.

> CP
> Respects to your father.

CP turns and exits.

INT. BEDROOM - NIGHT

CP sleeping. He is in nightmare mode. CP sweats, tosses, and turns. Entering his dream, Mrs. P is on her knee's bedside in deep prayer.

> MRS. P
> Dear Lord, please watch over my children. I beg You, Lord, to take care of Charles. He's a good boy deep down. Protect him, dear Jesus, from all hurt, harm, and danger—

Mrs. P's words overlap as to a visual remembrance of Daphanie, how beautiful she was, and then to her lying dead.

SCENES ARE REVISITED

CP watches as his father is shot.

Bobby China attempts to hold Daphanie's head in his lap.

The scene changes to the gunshot to Glen's head. The scene changes again to CP's remembrance of the county jail inmate Willie "on the new."

                    WILLIE
Y'all had pork chops yesterday, right?

INT. MOTEL BEDROOM - NIGHT

CP in bed. The phone rings. CP answers it.

                    CP
Yeah. All right. Connect it.

It's Barbara.

INT. BEDROOM - NIGHT

Barbara is on the phone, sitting in bed.

                  BARBARA
CP, you need to know right away that John's family has canceled whatever arrangement you had. The police are arresting you and other Blackstone leaders. They say you can avoid prison by joining the military by tomorrow. That's straight from Mr. Calabrese. Call me. Let me know what you decide. I'll meet you.

INT. MOTEL - SAME NIGHT

CP hangs up the phone and thinks about the call and the decision he must make.

CP goes to his knees in prayer.

CP has decided. He gets dressed and leaves his weapon on a table. He exits the motel.

EXT. MOTEL - DAY

CP notices two young red beret-wearing Satan Lovers in front of the motel.

> CP
>
> Young brothers!

THE YOUNG SATAN LOVERS SALUTE.

> YOUNG SLS
>
> CHIEF!

> CP
>
> Flag me down a cab.

The young Satan Lovers break to the street and flag down a taxi. A taxi stops, and CP enters.

INT. TAXI - DAY

> TAXI DRIVER
>
> Where to?

> CP
>
> My father was Navy. You know that Navy Recruitment Office on Western Ave?

> TAXI DRIVER
>
> 71st and Western?

> CP
>
> Yeah, right there.

The driver makes a turn heading toward CP's destination.

EXT. STREET - DAY

Larry Russell and Kilman sitting in the rear of a parked auto. CP in the taxi passes them. Larry has no problem seeing CP endowed in his Black P. Stone uniform.

INT. AUTO STREET - SAME DAY

To Kilman

> LARRY
>
> You see that!

> KILMAN
>
> What's up?

> LARRY
>
> That punk-ass Satan Lover that killed my brother is in that cab. Come on!

Larry beckons his driver to get back in the car.

> LARRY
>
> Catch up with that cab!

The car doors are closed. The driver takes off after the taxi.

INT. AUTO - SAME DAY

Larry pulls his 38-caliber pistol from his waist and makes sure it's loaded.

> LARRY
>
> Pull up behind him when he stops at the light.

The taxi stops at a traffic light. As if well rehearsed, Kilman and Larry exit their vehicle, weapons drawn, approach the taxi, and open the front and rear doors like clockwork.

INT. TAXI - DAY

> LARRY
> Don't reach for it, CP! Driver move over if you don't want to die!

The taxi driver puts his hands up and slides over. CP also does as ordered.

To taxi driver

> KILMAN
> Get out the car, man.

The taxi driver moves speedily. He exits the taxi. He stands outside the vehicle until motioned by Kilman to walk away.

To Kilman

> LARRY
> Pull in that alley on 69th street.

The taxi pulls off followed by Larry's car.

> LARRY
> Don't move, CP. It don't matter to me where we at when I take your life. Make a wrong move, and I do what um gonna do anyway.

Larry keeps his gun pointed at CP. He searches for CP's weapon. He finds nothing.

> CP
> Naw, man. No pistol. I was getting out of this today, man. Joining the military.

> LARRY
> Yeah, but it's the war here in Chicago you ain't gonna survive.

To Kilman

> LARRY
> Pull in here!

Kilman and the following auto quickly pull into an alley.

To Kilman

> LARRY
> Get on out, man. I'll meet you on Halsted Street in a couple of hours.

Larry watches Kilman get into the auto behind the taxi and then drive off.

> LARRY
> Be sure to say hello to my brother, CP.

> CP
> Yeah, he forgives you for leaving him, and my father forgives me.

Larry points his pistol closer to CP's head, hoping to stimulate fear.

Larry gets out of the car.

                    LARRY
Get out! Damn! Killing you gonna feel good!

CP, still resigned, exits the vehicle.

                    CP
Killing you would've felt good too. But I feel different now. I repent of everything I've done wrong.

                    LARRY
Damn, you got heart, or you done loss your mind, boy! Come on, let's do this face to face.

Larry pulls the hammer back, cocking his pistol. CP closes his eyes.

                    CP
I got my mother's prayers! Thank you, Ma!

Larry pulls the trigger. Nothing. He continues pulling the trigger. Nothing. Somehow, each round misfires. It's a miracle. CP's eyes open. He is the most surprised.

                    LARRY
What! How!

CP slowly examines himself. There's no blood. He looks up.

                    CP
Thank You, Jesus.

                    CP
Larry looks at his weapon and again takes aim. He cocks the hammer when a well-placed bullet hits his upper body. Eyes wide open, a stare of confusion and disbelief is easily read. He falls.

Chicago Police detective Edward Buchannon stands yards away, having used the top of his unmarked police car to steady his aim. He approaches CP.

> OFFICER EDWARD BUCHANNON
> We been watching you, making sure you took our offer to join the military.

> OFFICER BANKS
> Yeah, thank Jesus. That was a miracle. Damn, you're pretty lucky.

> OFFICER EDWARD BUCHANNON
> CP, keep your luck going. Take the taxi, and go protect our country.

CP shakes his head in disbelief, gets behind the wheel of the taxi, and drives off.

EXT. US NAVY ENLISTMENT OFFICE - DAY

CP and Barbara walk toward the entrance of a US Naval enlistment office. They embrace.

EXT. NIGHT REAR OF THE USS MIDWAY AIRCRAFT CARRIER CVA 41

CP stands at the rear of an aircraft carrier, looking at the open sea.

FADE OUT

The End

About the Author

Calvin "Champagne" Powell is an actor, vocalist, songwriter, novelist, and screenwriter. Mr. Powell grew up on Chicago's Southside in the violent and legendary neighborhood of Englewood. Mr. Powell survived the 1960s Chicago Disciple-Black P. Stone war. In 1971 he enlisted in the US Navy during the Vietnam conflict. In 1978, he obtained a bachelor of arts degree in theater from Columbia College, Chicago. In 1981, Mr. Powell was awarded the prestigious Joseph Jefferson Award for his performance in *The Mighty Gents*. He has appeared in numerous theater, film, and TV productions. In 1985, Mr. Powell was replaced by an upcoming Denzel Washington in the Broadway production of "Checkmates." Mr. Powell was also a social worker for the State of Illinois and the Chicago Youth Centers, servicing the Cabrini Green Projects. Mr. Powell in 2021 retired from Los Angeles County's Department of Children and Family Services, performing duties as an emergency response investigator. Now at seventy-three, Mr. Powell remains married to his wife of twenty years, Barbie, with a fifty-three-year-old son and five adult stepchildren.

Printed in the USA
CPSIA information can be obtained
at www.ICGtesting.com
CBHW031531121024
15708CB00038B/559